THE ALCHEMY OF BECOMING

TESTIMONIALS

"Helpful, bright, and encouraging! Tiffany's energy shines through on every page. Her framework has helped me personally to take steps toward real and significant change"

~ Heidi K., Indiana

"Thank you! Reading your books has inspired me to listen better to my intuition. What you do for others is truly a blessing."

~ Jessica W., Texas

"I didn't know muscle testing was this easy!"

~ Jordie W., Utah

"Muscle testing was a new concept for me, and I think Tiffany prefaced it well and then described it well. What an amazing way to navigate through life's many options, choices, emotions, and problems! Tiffany has a gift for healing and such a calm spirit in her work and service towards others."

~ Robin M., Hawaii

"Learning the basics of muscle testing has helped me grow. Thank you, Tiffany."

~ Samantha S., Texas

"For years I've been muscle testing through trials, illnesses, and goals. This book is about so much more than mere muscle testing. I am more fully aware of the blessings around me, my intuition has been strengthened, and I have a better understanding of my place in this world."

~ Sarah J., Texas

"'Irreducible self' are two words in this book that connected me with a power to evaluate my life and choose to become my best self. I'm learning to ask 'discerning questions,' move my life forward in a meaningful way, help my children better, and get closer to crossing that 'healing finish line.' Thank you, Tiffany, for all your work to help me and thousands of others!"

~ Julie V., Idaho

"While it is an invaluable skill to learn, muscle testing is only the beginning. Tiffany invites you to live more fully and bravely into your life, to face your fears, integrate your shadow, and whittle your 'little self' down to nothing but a whisper—if not silence it altogether."

~ Shane T., Indiana

THE ALCHEMY OF BECOMING

MUSCLE TESTING
FOR SELF-DISCOVERY

TIFFANY GARVIN

Silver Torch Press
Beverly Hills, CA

The Alchemy of Becoming: Muscle Testing for Self-Discovery

Copyright © 2021 by Tiffany Garvin

www.TiffanyGarvin.com
www.ServeLoveLift.com
LifeAboveTheLine@gmail.com

Published by Silver Torch Press
www.SilverTorchPress.com
jill@SilverTorchPress.com

Trade Paperback ISBN: 978-1-950370-13-9
eBook ISBN: 978-1-950730-14-6
Library of Congress Catalog Number: 2021901620

Cover image and design by Tiffany Garvin.
Edited by Shane Thomson.

Printed in the United States of America.

"It doesn't matter where you are coming from. All that matters is where you are going."

~ Brian Tracy

CONTENTS

CONTENTS

ACKNOWLEDGMENTS

The beautiful response of this book has inspired me. I know it's because of the love that went into its creation along with the desire to serve and lift all who read its pages. The credit belongs to several remarkable people...

Shane, I'm so grateful for your depth of understanding of the material as you edited this book. Your gifts of love, writing, and breathing life into others has helped this book to penetrate people's hearts.

Sarah, thank you for your constant support and belief in me. Your heart is gold, and your friendship is a treasure.

Sterling, Connery, and Keeley, you keep me on my toes and motivate me to do a little better every day and become a better mom for you.

Dad, I'm so grateful for your steady love and epic cheerleading throughout my life. Your tenacity became my own, and it saved me. You're my hero, and I love you so much!

Mom, it has been a blessing to be your daughter. Even though you're my guardian angel now, watching me from the other side, I feel your love still and hope I'm making you proud.

Chris, thank you so much for the endless support, inspired brainstorming sessions, and help with keeping my sanity. God knew my heart needed you. Your love has given me wings to fly, and they'll always lead me back to you. I love you forever!

Reader, thank you for choosing this book. Know that I wrote it with the intention to lift and empower you to grow and overcome your challenges. I believe you have beautiful gifts and a powerful purpose that you're meant to serve our world with. I desire for you to experience this remarkable *alchemy*, to become the best version of yourself, and experience true, lasting joy!

FOREWORD

Some of the biggest things in our lives can come in small, unexpected packages. For me, that little package was a young boy with leukemia. His name was Chris, and even though I only knew him for a few days, he changed my life.

Chris's heroes were police officers, especially Ponch and Jon from the hit TV show "CHiPs." The only thing he wanted more than to keep living was to be a motorcycle officer like them. Along with other officers of the Arizona Highway Patrol, I helped to grant his wish. Chris became the first and only honorary Highway Patrol officer, complete with a tiny, custom-made uniform, trooper's hat, badge, and motorcycle uniform wings.

For a few precious moments, Chris was just a normal kid again. His mother beamed as he ran around free and happy, playing on the police motorcycles and living his wish to the fullest. He passed away only a few days later.

My life had not been the easiest, and my challenges had taken a toll on me. But meeting Chris changed me and something shifted inside. He was my inspiration to create and co-found the Make-A-Wish Foundation, a non-profit that grants wishes to children around the world who have life-threatening illnesses. I had finally found my purpose.

Who knows but that the little thing you need to change your life will be found in the pages of this special book. Tiffany has poured out her heart, sharing profound wisdom that can help transform your challenges into growth opportunities and your heartbreak into life-changing wisdom.

Tiffany and I met a few years ago at an event in Los Angeles where I was speaking about the upcoming film *Wish Man*. She was a lovely young lady and a bestselling author with a bright future. Since that time, she has continued to coach and empower countless people to improve their physical, mental, and emotional health. Her mission is to serve, love, and lift people so that they can do the same for others wherever they are.

She is making a real difference in people's lives, and this book continues that work. Too many people are struggling under the weight of their challenges. Tiffany gives you step-by-step guidance with her pioneering strategies and techniques to overcome your burdens and come closer to becoming the best version of yourself. Her encouraging tone instills belief and hope in the possibility of a greater future.

I encourage you to avail yourself of the gift of life and vitality she offers you here.

FRANK SHANKWITZ
Creator and Co-founder of the Make-A-Wish Foundation
www.WishMan1.com

Author's Note: In the time between his writing this foreword and this book's being published, Mr. Shankwitz passed away. I guess that means that among the last wishes he granted was mine. Thank you, Frank.

INTRODUCTION

What is life but a series of experiences that challenge us, nurture us, and point us to who we can become? Family, friends, and even strangers all play a role in this production—our life production. All of the ups and downs, triumphs and trials, perform their dance around us and within us as we respond to each one.

As we choose to face, learn from, and overcome our challenges again and again, a kind of magic infuses our journey and begins to transform us. We leave behind our original stature and move toward the ultimate potential of our very being. This course that refines us is a beautiful alchemy meant to purify us from the weaknesses, wounds, and impurities we collect along our path.

I recently heard an inspired definition of alchemy. It went something like this:

Alchemy is the process by which we remove all of the elements and alloys that we have accumulated throughout our lives until all that remains after being held over constant heat, over eons of time, is the irreducible Self, the very essence of who we are.

This process of alchemy can be facilitated by the skill of muscle testing, which is a powerful method for tapping into the body's wisdom. With this ability, guided by thoughtful questions, we can discover helpful and insightful truths about ourselves that can lead us to greater health, happiness, and success.

Muscle testing was the catalyst for a miraculous phase of my own *alchemy of becoming*, a phase that began in early 2014, shortly after I turned 40. At that time muscle testing seemed like a new concept to me, but looking back, I realized it had been part of my life since I was young.

I recall at least two memorable experiences with muscle testing from my youth. One was with a chiropractor who would ask me to hold my arm straight out so she could test and evaluate my skeletal alignment. Telling me to resist, she would press down on my arm to see if it moved. Sometimes it held strong, sometimes it dropped easily, and the results of those muscle tests informed her treatments. I have since learned that many practitioners use this "arm-lever" method of muscle testing in their work, as it is a type of biofeedback tool that can provide information about the inner workings of the body, heart, mind, and spirit. (I'll actually teach you a form of it later in this book!)

The other experience I had of seeing muscle testing in action was at a personal development event with one of my favorite speakers: my dad. Among other things, my amazing dad spoke professionally, and in one of his presentations used that same arm-lever method of muscle testing in a way that was both instructive and entertaining. He taught groups of young adults about the power of intention, and part of his presentation included a kind of muscle testing "parlor trick" using a big, strong guy from the audience.

My dad asked the volunteer to hold an arm straight out and then, telling him to resist, practically hung on the guy's arm. Dad was pretty strong himself, but he was never able to force the arm down. He then told the audience he was going to "split" the young man's aura, which would weaken the arm so he could easily pull it down.

This was met with chuckles and scoffs, especially as Dad assumed his best karate stance and cut an imaginary line with his hand from the guy's head to his toes. To the surprise of the audience—and the young man—Dad pushed his arm down to his side...with one finger! Everyone's eyes went wide with astonishment.

Far more impressive than the awe factor of his demonstration was that he was applying real principles of muscle testing, something neither of us realized at the time. Moreover, neither of us could know then how important this would become later in my life.

In the mid 90's, I was an active and energetic young adult, when I suddenly became sick with multiple chronic illnesses. At that time no one truly understood conditions like fibromyalgia and chronic fatigue syndrome. They were mysterious ailments that doctors could hardly diagnose, let alone treat effectively. I was told that my condition—debilitating pain, oppressive fatigue, mental fog, and other such symptoms—was basically a life sentence. Others said there was nothing they could do but try to manage the symptoms through medications. It wasn't a promising outlook, particularly since the meds didn't really help.

I believed I could get well somehow, though the search for solutions felt like an impossible treasure hunt. My parents took me to all kinds of alternative therapists hoping to find answers. While a few of the treatments provided some temporary relief, the pain always returned. I held on to hope, but I began to doubt that anyone could actually help me. I felt powerless.

Then, in early 2014, my hopes were rewarded. I learned this remarkable skill of muscle testing and some simple healing techniques and started experimenting. As I applied these new skills, a miracle happened: the pain started going away, *and it was through my own efforts.* After 18 long, exhausting years, I finally felt some power over my health challenges. I had been in the dark for so long, not knowing where to go or what to do to find relief. Then, suddenly, sunlight broke through the clouds and I knew the journey had shifted. I had entered into a new, profound course toward healing.

Since then, I have come to learn what a wonderful tool muscle testing can be to provide valuable understanding about our wellbeing. It changed the course of my life as I uncovered the mysteries lying beneath my chronic illnesses. From emotional wounds to limiting subconscious paradigms, I learned what was preventing my body from healing and what to do to overcome those obstacles.

Through muscle testing I was empowered to identify how to support my body in its natural healing efforts. I tested for which essential oils I needed, for example, or which supplements to take and when. I continued to use muscle testing as I employed various healing techniques and watched as my life transformed.

The information I learned and guidance I discerned led me down a path to healing that doctors had said was impossible. After 18 years of struggle, I overcame my chronic illnesses and began living a new, freer life.

(I talk more about my healing journey in my bestselling book *Life Above the Line: Living the Life You're Meant to Live.* In it I share the mindset, principles, stepping stones, and techniques I used to cross that healing finish line. I will share one of those techniques later in this book.)

Another game changer was learning how to ask powerful questions, making it possible to move my life forward in new and meaningful ways. The usefulness of muscle testing is amplified when we ask effective questions. They help us see underlying truths, explore greater possibilities, and deeply improve the quality of our lives.

As we progress through this book together, I will share many examples that illustrate how to ask great questions. You too can gain these skills, find answers to your challenges, and move your life forward.

****

We each have reasons for wanting to learn muscle testing. For me it was a long, significant health crisis, but I know that muscle testing can facilitate more than just physical and emotional healing. It can be a means of gaining insights into every aspect of our lives: physical and mental health, career, personal fulfillment, and supporting our families and loved ones in their personal and professional challenges.

What is it for you? What are you facing in your life? What answers are you seeking?

Maybe you're craving to know your purpose in life or feeling nudged to add more meaning to your days. Do you have a career choice to make, a business opportunity to consider, or a decision about what to study in college? Perhaps you are struggling with an important relationship, such as with your spouse, children, co-worker, money, or even yourself.

Whatever your challenges and whatever mysteries you need answers to, the principles in this book can guide you. That's my whole purpose in writing it: to help you gain powerful skills to access truth, grow, overcome your trials, and achieve your goals. I believe you were born to do great things!

I invite you to open your heart as you read through these pages. You can be a powerful force for good as you overcome your challenges, move through your own *alchemy of becoming*, and gain the freedom to live the life you're meant to live.

PART 1

"Create your future from your future, not your past."

~ Werner Erhard

CHAPTER 1

Why Muscle Test

I wish every person in the world could muscle test. Imagine going through life empowered to discover key insights into your needs, the needs of those you care for, and being able to access your innermost truths so you can overcome your greatest challenges. Muscle testing can be the key to acquiring that powerful information. Through muscle testing, there's no more wondering what's going on physically, mentally and emotionally, or what the next steps are—you can just ask!

Life's difficulties can overwhelm us as we try to figure out what we need to overcome them or where to even start. Some people have the gift of a refined, clear sense of intuition and can easily perceive what they need, but most of us are not like that. In this way, muscle testing becomes a very helpful tool to gain insight and direction.

Muscle testing is a means to an end. It's a skill that, when combined with the skill to ask valuable questions, can dramatically improve the quality of your life. If you're just here for the skill to muscle test, that's fine. We will educate your mind, strengthen your confidence, and increase your clarity. I hope you will also be open to the ideas, principles and practices in this book that can have a much greater impact on your health, joy, purpose, and success as well.

Consider the vast variety of physical ailments—sicknesses, migraines, weight issues, chronic illnesses, injuries, food and environmental reactions, and more. Such afflictions can stop us in our tracks, leading us to seek help from a long list of resources, such as doctors, nutritionists, self-help books, gurus, fitness trainers, alternative therapists, and so on.

Then there are the mental and emotional challenges that can be just as paralyzing—anxiety, depression, chronic stress, self-sabotage, negative thought patterns, and even lack of financial success. These issues are not all helped by medication or motivational speakers. Often they are rooted in unresolved trauma, inherited subconscious programs, and other internal blocks. The invisible nature of many of these difficulties can make them feel impossible to overcome.

What if you could learn how to tap into what your body really needs, not just what experts think is your answer—as intelligent and informed as they may be? Your problems are your own and unique to your circumstances and experiences. What may cure or solve another person's issue could be totally wrong for you. Their struggle to overcome their issue could be caused by illness or chronic stress, while yours could be an underlying emotion or inherited pattern. Different root causes need different solutions.

Let's look specifically at an example of trying to lose weight. A couple I have worked with both had moderate but meaningful weight loss goals. They had tried to lose weight before but had struggled to find something they could really stick with. They wanted something more customized to their particular strengths and weaknesses.

The first step was simply to ask a question: In order to lose weight, what do you feel like you need to do first? The husband felt impressed to learn some exercise and diet strategies from a trusted friend. We muscle tested through the different exercise programs and found one that tested strong as a good place to start. We also muscle tested through options for tracking his food and caloric intake. After identifying the best strategies for him to begin with, he committed to an incremental plan that felt possible.

He started by tracking his food and using muscle testing to identify what foods and portions were best for him throughout each day. A couple of weeks later it was time to begin the exercise program, and he used muscle testing to help identify and adjust his food needs based on the increased activity. Muscle testing increased his confidence in his choices and, when he sensed something was off, helped him make smooth in-course corrections.

The wife's path was different. As she contemplated her situation, she perceived that her struggle to lose weight was emotional. Through muscle testing we confirmed this was indeed the case. While she did choose to be more conscious with her diet and incorporate more activity when she could, she focused her efforts on her impression to love people more. That's right, she felt inspired that the keys to lowering her weight were to be more patient with her family, to love people around her (even those that were difficult to love), and to hold a spirit of love in her mind and heart constantly.

It didn't take long for this approach to start getting results. After only a month, they were both already halfway to their goal weights and their momentum was strong. Their blocks to weight loss were unique to them, so they both needed very different approaches to resolving their weight concerns. Muscle testing augmented their intuition, helped them uncover the best strategies for their individual needs, and led them along uniquely successful paths—which was exactly what they needed!

Wouldn't it be wonderful if everyone in the world had access to this kind of customization? It's almost as good as having your own personal owner's manual. So often people struggle with solving their problems because they are applying other people's solutions instead of identifying and addressing the nature and needs of their own situations.

Food allergies represent another difficult physical challenge. One of my students had been an alternative health and wellness practitioner for many years and was very skilled in her work. She had been able to eliminate nearly all of her food reactions, but she hadn't been able to resolve her issues with dairy.

I walked her through muscle testing several questions to identify the source of her reaction to dairy until we discovered something curious.

Some of the questions we tested through were:

- Is the root cause of this reaction to dairy physical? The answer was *no*.

- Is the root cause of the reaction emotional? The answer was *yes*.

- Is there a message behind this issue? *Yes*.

After a moment, she recalled the traumatic experience of one of her grandparents. We tested and confirmed that this was indeed the root cause of her reactions. This trauma had been passed down through DNA to her, and it manifested as a physical ailment.

We spent a few minutes making sure we understood everything we needed to know about the new awareness. Then, using the principles and techniques from my book *Life Above the Line*, we worked through the issue until it was resolved. When muscle testing indicated there was nothing left to work through, we tested to see whether the root cause had been resolved, and we tested *yes*. That night after class, she was able to eat and enjoy ice cream for the first time in years!

There's a great deal we can learn from this story, but the main point for us to remember here is that sometimes our challenges are made up of surprising elements. We can't always guess what is causing our difficulties, so knowing how to muscle test and ask good questions can literally be life changing.

It's also important to remember that muscle testing doesn't take the place of researching and gathering important information. We learn all we can from wise and reliable sources and analyze what we find to understand as best we can what we've learned. Then, we narrow down those options with muscle testing to determine the best options for us and go make the change. This creates an environment for discerning important variables with greater accuracy to support us in decision-making, and ultimately greater health and success.

There really are an infinite number of personal and professional issues that muscle testing can help us resolve. We can identify why we sabotage ourselves while moving toward goals. We can understand why we get anxious in certain situations. We can discover and work through the blocks preventing us from feeling peaceful, being financially strong, and achieving our dreams.

Muscle testing can not only provide answers to these types of questions and mysteries, it can also build our confidence knowing we're taking the most effective actions and making the best choices for ourselves. It can even help us care for those we love.

How amazing would it be if parents could discern what their children need, especially when they can't verbalize it? From nutrition to sleep to a listening ear or snuggles, we can understand what our children lack, and we can respond in ways that address the *actual* need and help them feel validation, love, and peace. And when we *really* understand what our children are feeling, it creates a beautiful tolerance and patience within us.

Muscle testing truly is a tool to help us change and create our lives. It can help us make decisions with more clarity and confidence. It can help us better access our truths, understand who we are, and realize our potential. It can help us recognize the mysteries behind our challenges so we can move through them with greater efficacy.

Muscle testing can help us own our power to make positive changes in our lives. It can help us move from swirling around beneath the line of survival to living in growth mode above it. This special tool can help us live our lives with more purpose and clearer intentions.

This book will teach you how to muscle test and begin identifying things that can be helpful in your day to day life. But, as you may have gathered, it won't stop there. There's so much more!

CHAPTER 2

Framework for Real Change

The simple goal of this book is to teach you the skill of muscle testing, and we'll get into that in a bit. The bigger vision of this book, however, is to help you create real change in your life. So, I think it's helpful to "begin with the end in mind," as Stephen R. Covey put it, and conceive a grander—and practical —vision of what you can accomplish as you develop your abilities.

I believe life has a purpose, and it facilitates opportunities for us to learn, grow, and become who we are meant to become so we can do what we are meant to do. As we learn all we can from the things we experience, we can make marvelous changes in our lives that help us to be happier, healthier, and more fulfilled.

These opportunities are often masked as our challenges. When we struggle and work hard to resolve difficult experiences, we change. We become stronger and more capable of facing future challenges and help others through theirs. As we submit ourselves to the process of learning and growing, we lift ourselves and inspire those around us.

Even when we are willing to learn and grow from our challenges, it can be difficult to know where to start. Frameworks can provide a clearer vision of our path ahead and behind us, and guide us through a maze of questions to find answers that teach important concepts.

Frameworks also give structure to our efforts to restore and maintain wellbeing and further personal development, while leading us through important processes to create real results. The framework I want to share with you is the Journey Framework.

I have used this 3-step framework for many years to effectuate remarkable change in my life and in the lives of those I teach and coach. It has helped me learn valuable lessons and progress in ways I needed to grow so that I could finally heal and move forward with my life in a new, powerful way. Applying this 3-step framework to a variety of challenges can help you to create real change and success in every facet of life.

Journey Framework

1. **Face the challenge** - Know what you're dealing with. You can muscle test through resources—books, important lists, foods—to identify factors contributing to your issue.

2. **Learn the lesson** - Learn what the challenge is trying to teach you. Evaluate the factors to understand what it all means to you.

3. **Make the change** - Do what is necessary to move forward. Shift a behavior or an environment or resolve an internal obstacle in order to overcome the challenge.

Quite often, we may find ourselves rushing through life or living on autopilot. We get out of bed, get ready, get the kids to school, maybe eat breakfast, and get to work. But when do we breathe? When do we actually live? What does it mean to really live anyway? When do we quiet our minds to listen to our life and what it's trying to tell us?

Our challenges are often relegated to speed bumps and annoyances that we try to quickly move past to get on with our busy lives. We don't feel like we have the bandwidth to think very deeply about a challenge to resolve it; we can hardly slow our frantic pace of checking off to-do's just to stay afloat.

This approach is what sets our lives up for crisis. This is waiting for the metaphorical brick to hit us in the head and demand our attention before we will prioritize it. While it may seem uncomfortable or time consuming to allow ourselves space to acknowledge our problems, hear the instructive and enlightening whispers of life's challenges, and make necessary changes, it will actually be less painful and more efficient in the end.

By honoring our challenges and seeking to work through them consciously, we engage in the *alchemy of becoming* that can turn trials into inspired changes and weaknesses into strengths.

Face the Challenge

When we *face the challenge*, we are taking the time to understand it. We slow our pace sufficiently to ask the questions necessary to identify what's really going on, which allows us to consciously and intentionally consider how to respond to it.

Using muscle testing can be a great way to begin discovering the pieces that make up the challenges we face. We can ask questions about things that we perceive are involved and get clarity about how accurate our perceptions are. We can test through our ideas and resources around us to gain simple, yet helpful, bits of information that lead us along the path to resolution.

We can be very adept at putting off this kind of internal work, and for good reasons! We may feel we don't have time, or believe it will be painful and want to avoid the discomfort. Perhaps we're already overwhelmed and feel like there's nothing we can do about it anyway. Or maybe we are simply afraid to face it. Whatever the resistance, it truly is better to face the problem now rather than neglect it and risk the current issue becoming a much larger, more difficult problem.

One sign that someone has deferred engaging in this type of helpful process for too long is that their behavior changes. I've seen this firsthand many times, and very recently with my husband. He has given me permission to share this story, realizing that it may be helpful for someone else who has faced a similar challenge and struggled with how to resolve it.

Chris is normally a very kind, loving person, but one day he was really grumpy. It seemed to come out of nowhere, and whatever was bothering him had festered into some real anger. When I brought it to his attention, he only got more upset, so I let him have some space to work through it on his own.

Later that night, I checked in with him again, and he was still very agitated. His words became more bitter and attacking the more we talked, so I knew something was really wrong. He can usually calm himself down and resolve things if he gets upset. This was clearly a bigger issue.

As he unloaded his frustrations about something that had happened earlier in the day, he seemed to be getting even more angry. I realized that he must be really hurting for him to behave this way, so I shifted my comments and questions from seeking an explanation for his grumpiness toward seeking to understand his pain.

As I made this conscious shift, I saw something change in him. He no longer felt he had to defend himself. He could sense a safe space to honestly explore what was going on inside of him. He told me about some painful things an old friend of his had posted on social media, how he felt like he was failing at his responsibilities as a provider for his family, and how some important goals seemed to be slipping through his fingers.

It was clear that a few concerns had been building up for a while and were triggered by a couple of events that day. Several factors had compounded the burdens he was feeling. The negative thoughts and stories coupled with the powerlessness he felt to change these circumstances were spiraling him downward.

Because of this internal battle, every new hard thing was exaggerated and his reactions amplified. He also realized that he hadn't questioned or challenged the negative thoughts he was having, so they were able to multiply and keep him in a heavy place.

The more I patiently listened, the calmer he became. The more compassion I showed—instead of staying offended at his behavior—the more he could let go of the wounds that were holding him hostage.

I don't mean to show myself as some magnanimous being here. Rather, I want to illustrate how deeply unaddressed concerns can build up and take over who we are for a time, and how we can each be a safe place for someone to feel heard, understood, and thus able to let go of their destructive baggage.

The more compassion we can feel for each other when we're not in our best moments and the more patience we can offer to each other when we're struggling, the more space we create for each other to experience healing.

During this discussion with my sweetheart, I quietly asked questions on his behalf, seeking answers with muscle testing for how to respond to him. I wanted to know when to just listen and let him talk, even when it was uncomfortable for me. I wanted to know what I could say to help him work through these burdens. Because I could use muscle testing through this experience, I didn't feel reactive. I could calmly listen and gain insights into what was really going on. I could be more loving and patient while he processed his feelings.

So many times we get offended when someone is grumpy with us. Whether it's the drive-thru guy or the gal checking us out at the grocery store, or even a close friend, sometimes our "stuff" just boils over and we have to let it out. Ideally, we do it when we won't hurt someone. Even better, we face our struggles early on so they don't build up. Either way, it's good to remember that someone else's behavior is not about us; just like when we struggle, it's not really about them.

Sometimes the process of discovery that comes with *facing the challenge* is enough to identify a quick solution and resolve the issue. Sometimes, however, there's more for us to understand. That's where step two comes in.

Learn the Lesson

After we gather the pieces of information that tell us what we're really facing in our challenge, we can begin to *learn the lesson* behind it. We can understand what it means to us and why we should pay attention.

Learning the lesson, or understanding the message behind our struggles, gives them meaning and purpose. Without this, our trials can seem pointless—even like torture. When I was sick for all those years, it seemed that there was no point to the persistent pain and frustrating fatigue, a perception that made them so much harder to tolerate.

However, when I began to understand how my difficulties were changing me, helping me become a better person, and teaching me remarkable things, I could handle them much better. They were no longer meaningless—they were miraculous.

Through my experiences, I've learned that life has beautiful lessons to teach us if we will listen. It can be pretty determined to teach those lessons, so it's better to learn them sooner than later. Listening for life's lessons even when they're hiding inside our challenges can open the door to profound growth and healing.

Sometimes life is knocking on the door, trying desperately to get our attention and move us out of our current trajectory. It can also be trying to lift us out of our comfortable misery that's leading us nowhere—or nowhere good.

Do yourself a favor and listen to the whispers telling you to pay more attention to your child, to build that relationship now, and to cherish the small moments.

Listen to your body when it tells you to slow down and breathe through the stress instead of pushing it down deeper to fester. Let it guide you on a path to physical and mental health instead of illness. It knows how to help you heal if you will learn how to listen.

Not giving ourselves the time and space to *learn the lessons* from our challenges can cause life to intensify its efforts and demand that we listen and learn. The resulting challenge can bring life to a halt if we defer the lessons long enough—things such as the loss of a job, becoming seriously ill, having a breakdown (can you say mid-life crisis?), and many other very real and difficult scenarios.

Chris learned that night that life was trying to help him remember to face his challenges and address his concerns when they arise. He knows how to work through them, but because he didn't feel like he could take the time to resolve them, he neglected them and they compounded. He learned again just how important it is to question those negative stories that try to pull us in.

We took the time together to process what he was feeling so he could *learn the lesson* he needed in that moment. He was willing to hear the lesson, and he recognized where he could listen sooner to prevent a bigger issue in the future.

Life is about learning and growing. These growth experiences can bring us joy and success if we can work through them effectively. If we skip over the learning and growing because we don't have the time or feel it's too hard, in a way we're not really living. Fortunately—or unfortunately—life will not give up trying to teach us its lessons. It will just show up in a different pair of pants or a bigger issue that we can't ignore anymore.

Muscle testing can be very helpful when processing thoughts and impressions that come as we're *learning the lessons* of life. When we can navigate this information effectively, we can more easily embrace the ideas that are true and good for us and steer clear of those that are harmful. Through this process we can gain confidence in learning life's valuable lessons and feel optimistic about making positive changes.

Make the Change

Once we know the contributing factors of the challenge we're facing and learn the lesson it's trying to teach us, we can discover what change we need to make and begin moving forward. The change may be external or internal.

The external change has to do with our interactions with our environment. It can be our relationships with family, friends, or co-workers. It might be a behavior or a habit. Maybe it's about our reactions to food, nature, or stress. The change may even have something to do with exercise—or the lack thereof.

The shifts we need to make come in all shapes, sizes, and levels of difficulty. Perhaps we find ourselves continually dropping things, the lesson in that could be that we need to get to bed earlier. Maybe there's a message in our feeling fatigued that's telling us to eat less sugar. Or possibly the random elbow pain could be suggesting a more complicated change, like needing to spend less time around a friend who is a negative influence. Whatever the change, the more willing we are to act on the invitation, the more effectively we can move through challenges.

Using muscle testing to help identify external changes can save a ton of time, money, and emotional effort experimenting. We can more easily narrow down the seemingly endless options to isolate the best way to make the necessary change. We can test through different theories about weight loss, for example, to know which ones are relevant to our specific needs. Or we can test to determine which marketing strategy to employ first for our business.

The change we need to make can be about pretty much anything in or around us. It could be about any one of a myriad of internal issues as well—resolving emotional burdens, negative thoughts, past traumas, or limiting beliefs.

Internal changes typically have to do with things we can't see as easily. They are the more mental and emotional factors contributing to our difficulties. These need a different approach; they need an internal shifting or healing approach.

There are many methods out there that can help us make these internal changes. If you have one you like, try using muscle testing to help you know when you've identified the right thing to resolve. Test to know how intense of an influence it has, and test to know when you've resolved all you can for it.

If you don't have a method for emotional releasing, shifting energy, or overcoming mental blocks, don't worry, you can use the techniques I teach in my book *Life Above the Line*. I will walk you through one of the techniques later in this book.

At this point you may be wondering how things fared with my husband's concerns. Well, by the next morning, the anger was mostly gone and he felt a bit lighter. He went on with his day, moving toward his goals, trying to focus on the positive things around him, and working to resolve the underlying issues that had boiled up.

Because he felt heard and validated and was able to express what had been bottled up, he could breathe and give these concerns the clear-headed attention they needed: He consciously chose to work through them. He dismissed the negative thoughts that tried to pull him back in and resolved the emotions that needed to be released. And, he was willing to make the internal and external changes that were necessary to feel relief and gain strength to face the real challenges in front of him.

By the end of the day, he had successfully faced his concerns, learned the lessons life was trying to teach him in that moment, and made the changes he needed to make. He had used muscle testing along the way to identify the internal and external changes he could make. It is important to note that many of the things that had bothered him were still there, but he felt lighter, more peaceful, and more capable of managing life again.

Like Chris's experience, some of the challenges we face are just layered and complicated enough to take us into the crazy zone, while others are straight-up devastating. Thankfully, many of the other bumps we face in life can be much simpler—and even humorous.

The following story is in the latter category, and it provides a good, quick example of the process of working through this framework. I've tried to break it down into clear steps so you can see the process more easily.

Recently, I helped one of my clients work through an interesting challenge. The second toe on her right foot was cramping and pulling away from her big toe. This may seem odd—and it is—but not for this client. She often has unique issues that try to get her attention when she doesn't hear a message in a subtler way. It definitely makes for some fun sessions.

We jumped right into testing through a few questions:

Face the Challenge

- Is there something I need to understand about my second toe cramping and trying to separate from the big toe? *Yes.*

- She quickly had a thought come to mind: *It has to do with separation.*

- Do I need to know anything more about the issue itself? *Yes.*

- What else do I need to know? (We tested through a chart I'd created about areas of life.) *Something about gifts and purpose.*

- Another thought came to look up the definition of *purpose.* There were two definitions, and she had the impression to combine them. *Something about the reason why she creates and her intention behind it.*

- Are they separated subconsciously? *Yes.*

Learn the Lesson

- Is there a separation between my intention and something I'm creating? She thought about it for a moment. *It's in her writing, specifically the new novel she was starting.* In an earlier session she had learned that she needed to create a clear intention for each of her books, but she hadn't created one for this book yet— she just started writing it without one. We spent a couple of minutes identifying her intentions for writing the new book. Once complete, we tested that we could move on.

- Is there any other message I need to understand from this? *No.*

Make the Change

- Now, is there anything else I need to do *externally* to resolve the issue with my toe. *No.*

- Is there anything I need to do *internally* to help resolve the issue with my toe? *No.*

Once we arrived at this point—though it may seem strange to you, it's wonderfully normal in my world—the problem with her toes suddenly went away. The second toe was no longer trying to separate itself from the big toe, and the very painful cramping incident was resolved!

That is the beauty and simplicity of this work, and I never get tired of seeing it in action.

Now, you may be wondering how on earth we came up with all those questions. The truth is it's something that comes with practice. Also, I have been teaching and working with this particular client for a long time, and she has really honed her intuition. She has learned to listen to and identify her inspired thoughts as she asks questions, and those thoughts have helped her ask additional questions to resolve some unique challenges. The good news is that you can become skilled at this, too.

Listen to your thoughts when you're asking questions to see what surfaces. Then, ask and test through other questions based on what comes to mind. When it comes to muscle testing, there really are no stupid questions. Don't write off any question too quickly, even—and perhaps especially—if what you come up with seems odd. Those "odd" questions may be exactly what you need to get the answers you desire.

You've likely witnessed how unresolved challenges have the unfortunate tendency of showing up later in a different form. Muscle testing and asking good questions with the Journey Framework—Face the Challenge, Learn the Lesson, Make the Change—can help us end that cycle and move forward in life.

I use the Journey Framework every day to coach myself and others through a wide range of challenges. Through this process we come to understand what we're really facing, learn the messages that free us to move forward, and become empowered to make the changes we need to in order to reach our goals.

There's a great side benefit to our efforts: less "baggage." Life can be hard enough without carrying around the extra weight of unresolved problems. I believe that life is meant to be better than that, and the Journey Framework coupled with muscle testing helps bring truly joyful living within reach.

CHAPTER 3

Life Can Be Better

I said it before, but I believe it's worth repeating: I wish every person in the world could muscle test and have access to this level of understanding about themselves, their challenges, and the wonderful lessons life has to teach them. I can only imagine how this would change people—and the world!—for the better.

From my own experiences, and through the experiences of those I've worked with, I can see at least one thing very clearly —just how priceless it really is to access the deeper levels of truth and understanding about our wellbeing that muscle testing can provide. We can know more easily what foods, opportunities, thoughts, and education we should accept into our lives and entertain in our minds and hearts. Knowing what drives us, limits us, and makes us successful is just as accessible as learning which shampoo will help our hair be happiest.

Here's another very practical benefit: as you learn how to access these truths with clear questions and the simple skill of muscle testing, you can make decisions much more easily. Your life will be better because you can more easily sift through all the various options and opinions available to you, identify what is most important for you personally, and be confident in your decisions.

As amazing as the current information age is, it's also full of well-founded, yet contradictory, opinions and advice about what is best or right. It's even a struggle to find clear information about something as basic as what foods are healthy and not healthy, beyond the obvious sweets and such. In the noisy, information-rich yet wisdom-deficient world in which we live, learning how to filter through all the options around us is essential.

If you've ever done any research on the internet, you've seen just how broad and conflicting the opinions are, even by those who claim to be experts. Bread is good, but gluten is bad. Milk is good for you, but lactose is not!

The contradictions don't stop there. In personal development, many gurus encourage us to reach for the stars, while others say the key is to keep your feet solidly on the ground. Love what you do to have success, but actually that doesn't matter—just work hard. I mean smart.

It can be confusing, to say the least. While many things we bring into our lives are simply a question of preference, when we're really trying hard to do what is best for ourselves with finite time and resources, we want a trusted source to reliably help guide us to what is best. Muscle testing has become that for me.

Without muscle testing, the process of sifting through the chaos of ideas is one of trial and error. With muscle testing, we can clear away the confusion of ambiguity and identify what pieces of wisdom and research apply to our current, personal circumstances. It can help us determine for ourselves what is good—or not good—for our own health, wellbeing, and success.

Muscle testing empowers us to break down any difficult decision into pieces and understand more clearly what we're facing. Decisions become less emotional and more logical, thus making decisions to move forward in our lives becomes more possible. And because the solutions are customized to our individual needs, our decisions are better for us overall

Remember the couple that was working to lose weight that I mentioned in Chapter 1? They both had the same goal but very different needs regarding how to get there. Through muscle testing, they were able to quickly identify the path they needed to follow, narrow down the options to create a specific plan, and then go forward with confidence on what has resulted in a very successful and enjoyable journey.

One experience that the husband had provides a good example for how muscle testing can help with food. He noticed that he needed help with recovery after his workouts, so he went to the internet to look for advice. The search results were massive, so he compiled the information from a few articles and started muscle testing through the different options to see what was best for him. Within a few minutes, he had a list of the best foods and beverages to help his body recover. So empowering!

Here's a different kind of example: One client was having a difficult time making an important decision regarding her business. The decision pertained to an opportunity that could build helpful relationships, offer valuable training, and was with a large group of knowledgeable people. The benefits were obvious and plentiful.

However, the downsides were equally clear. Normally, a big event with up to 100 people wouldn't be an issue, but during the COVID-19 pandemic it was. And since some of her loved ones were considered "high risk" for complications, that could be a real problem. The polarity of the pros and cons made coming to an acceptable decision seem impossible.

We carefully identified each factor and began weighing them out. After a few minutes, she felt calm and clear-headed, and she realized that her first task was to obtain more information. From there, I coached her to use muscle testing to assess the personal benefits and risks of each factor on a scale of 1-10. After considering everything, she made an informed, well thought-out decision that helped her move forward feeling more peaceful and confident.

As we are able to obtain better information and understanding, our choices will not only be easier—they will be better. After all, when we know better, we do better. Muscle testing helps us gain that clarity by cutting through confusion, emotional biases and burdens, and other complicating factors.

Another common variable that can complicate decision-making is when the choice is wrapped up in our identity. Being able to know more clearly who we are and what is in alignment with our identity can help us recognize valuable opportunities when they present themselves. We can know if they are good for us because we can access those priceless truths about ourselves.

One client I worked with had been recently married and was feeling particularly troubled about transitioning from her maiden name. She loved the man and his family, so the concern wasn't about the name itself. Still, she struggled to understand the resistance she was feeling.

We walked through a series of questions to learn more about what was really going on, and the answers she received were eye-opening:

Face the Challenge

- Is there something I need to know about this issue? *Yes.*

- Is it in any of my resources? *Yes.* We tested through a list of areas of life for *purpose.* This concern had something to do with how she related to her purpose.

- Is there anything else I need to know about contributing factors? *No.*

Learn the Lesson

- Is there a message in this concern—a lesson I need to learn? *Yes.*

- How does giving up my maiden name relate to my purpose? She took a moment to listen. *She felt like her identity and purpose were integrally connected with her maiden name, not her married name.*

- Is that part of the lesson I need to understand? *Yes.*

- How are my identity and purpose connected with my maiden name instead of married name? She took another moment to listen and tested through thoughts that surfaced to find the one that was relevant here. *Because she got married in her late 20's, her maiden name felt more like her real identity, and her purpose was connected to that name, not her married name.*

- Is there anything else I can learn about this? *No.*

Make the Change

- Is there something I can do to help this? *Yes.*

- Externally? *No.*

- Internally? *Yes.* We tested through some lists regarding mental and emotional issues to find what needed to change. *We found that she needed to resolve the belief that her maiden-name identity and married-name identity were both her. The dreams, values, and opportunities from her early life also belong to her married life and who she is now.*

This was such a profound conversation. It made me think about how many of us have experienced something that has disconnected us from our identity. It also made me so grateful that we could identify these truths for her and resolve them. How many ways do you think this confusion could have limited this young woman throughout her life if it hadn't been discovered and resolved?

Many of the challenges and crises in our lives can be resolved much more quickly when we know how to address them properly. Muscle testing can be a powerful tool in these circumstances.

Our nephew was recently hospitalized with severe pneumonia for several weeks. The technology available today saved him by providing a clear picture of what was going on inside of his body. It helped the doctors identify the problem, determine what courses of action were most appropriate, monitor his progress, and see what adjustments needed to be made. The visibility into his body made all the difference in his treatment and recovery.

Similarly, when we use muscle testing properly, we gain an amazing kind of visibility into our mind, body, and spirit that guides us to what will help us address our challenges in the best way. We can identify the root cause, determine the best course of action, monitor our progress, and make adjustments along the path. Just as a small rudder can turn a large ship, this little skill of muscle testing can change the course of our lives in amazing ways.

I invite you to consider what issues you are dealing with that muscle testing might help you resolve. Do you have any persistent physical discomforts that you could begin to understand? Are there any stresses or feelings of anxiety that are ready to be resolved? Do you have any limiting beliefs holding you back from reaching some important goals?

With muscle testing and asking good questions, you can begin a treasure hunt that offers adventure, self-discovery, and remarkable possibilities for success. Life can always be better.

CHAPTER 4

What Muscle Testing Is and Is Not

Before we go any further, I want to be very clear about what muscle testing is—and what it is not. I do get a little technical here, but it's because I want you to really understand this great tool.

On a high level, muscle testing *is* a skill that can help us discover some of the mysteries in our lives regarding health, happiness, success, and overall personal wellbeing. The better our questions, the more valuable the information we can access.

Muscle testing *is not* divining our future or learning things that are not ours to know. Here's a quick overview.

Muscle Testing Is...	Muscle Testing Is Not...
Accessing truth	Mind reading
Based on our intention	Fortune telling
Empowering	Magical/Mystical
Scientific	Diagnostic

What Muscle Testing Is

Now let's go a bit deeper. Simply stated, muscle testing is the ability to tap into the information flowing through us, which is carried along our energy meridians and is available to help us. It's amazing to think that the answers to so many of our health and life mysteries are literally inside of us, just under the surface of our skin.

Our subconscious mind accesses this energetic flow of truths and acts as a bridge to our conscious mind. Our intention facilitates crossing this bridge to access what we need. It helps relay our questions. The energy flowing through our meridians is responsive to our intentions and delivers back to us specific answers in response to our questions.

On a quick side note, it's important to be clear what I mean by "truth." I believe there are two relevant kinds of truth: universal and situational. Universal truth is permanent and applies in all cases. Situational truth, while true in the moment, is subject to change as needs and circumstances change.

As a simple example, it's a universal truth that we all must eat to live, but each individual has their own situational truth about which foods and quantities are best for their body at a given time.

Going a little deeper, the value of human relationships is universal, but what needs to be part of that relationship to make it the best it can be for both parties is unique to each particular situation.

Through muscle testing we can identify both universal and situational truths. The freer we are from biases, prejudices, interfering belief patterns, etc., the more easily and clearly we can access truths of all kinds, understand how they impact us, and incorporate them into our lives.

The way we receive these answers is either through intuition or an external response tool such as muscle testing. The channel of communication or "parts" of the body that are involved in muscle testing are the subconscious mind, the inner network of energy pathways called meridians, and the muscles of whichever physical tool or muscle testing method we use.

The more our questions are honest, truth-seeking, and unbiased, the more accurately this system of communication can function and give helpful answers. If we impose our beliefs, opinions, or assumptions on this process we can easily short circuit the communication and produce false answers.

Keeping our biases in check helps us learn powerful truths and offers us direction to solve our challenges or make important decisions. Biases are essentially preconceived notions about how something is or ought to be. Sometimes fear, arrogance, or stubbornness can cause us to hold onto our biases, and that interference prevents muscle testing from being really accurate or helpful. Decide now to always pursue the truth when you test.

This process of open, honest seeking of information can strengthen our natural intuitive skills. As we practice receiving answers to our questions through muscle testing, we train our intuition to learn this process better. It becomes more in tune with this internal communication.

As you become more practiced, you may notice answers coming to your mind before you test for them. That's a good thing! The ultimate goal is that we hone our intuition through using the skill of muscle testing so we can know what is good for us even more easily and organically.

Muscle testing is also a tool to empower us in our wellness efforts. As I said before, this skill is a means to an end. It is a beautiful method for learning the valuable truths inside of us that can improve the quality of our lives—physically, mentally, emotionally, etc.

I love muscle testing because, with it, there are fewer occasions of feeling powerless. We can ask questions until we feel confident about how to move forward. We can learn to make decisions more quickly and easily. We can gain peace and clarity as we understand more about ourselves, our environment, and how to resolve our challenges. We can know the powerful truths about who we are and accomplish our purpose in this world.

What Muscle Testing Is Not

There are times when the scope of what muscle testing *is* and *is not* can become unclear. We can accidentally move into that gray area when seeking information about the best actions to take or decisions to make, where we are concerned about our interactions with others, and what *is* and *is not* ok to resolve internally with intentional healing. This skill is for helping us uncover the mysteries of our own wellness—our own health, happiness, and success—not for solving all the world's problems.

I have found that there are some very clear lines of distinction where using muscle testing becomes inappropriate. One of those lines we don't cross is using muscle testing to read someone's mind. Even if it could be done accurately and reliably—and I'm not convinced it can—it simply isn't ethical. What others think has nothing to do with you. How they behave may impact you, but their thoughts are theirs and are therefore private. You have no business trying to learn those secrets.

Second, muscle testing is also not to be used for predictive purposes, like fortune telling. Don't try to test for lottery numbers, to know your future, or to read someone else's future. It doesn't work that way. If someone tells you that it does, run the other direction. You don't want to be around that kind of energy.

Early on while learning how to muscle test and ask good questions, I sometimes fell into the trap of asking about the timing of things that could help solve some of my challenges. There were times when I felt like I got a clear answer about when to expect a certain event or outcome. What I didn't realize was that my earnest desire to know this information combined with my ignorance about the appropriate use of muscle testing would short circuit my ability to get real answers.

It was an honest mistake, but those biases caused me a bit of grief when the anticipated events didn't happen. My first reaction was to question both myself and my ability to muscle test. But I eventually learned that asking about the timing of things in the future was not within the scope of muscle testing. That's not the kind of information we're accessing.

I want to be clear here: Muscle testing is not predictive; however, it *can* take the future into account. For example, at times I have felt drawn to ideas or projects that didn't make sense at the moment. Being a somewhat pragmatic person, I can tend to "logic" myself away from those thoughts. But if I stop and muscle test to see if the random idea is actually the best thing to do, I will often get a *yes*, so I do it. And more often than not, my future self is glad I did!

Third, while muscle testing may seem mysterious to some, it is not a mystery, mystical, or magic. As cool and intriguing as muscle testing is, there's less glitz and glam to it than that. It is a scientific method based on applied kinesiology, and it can be explained through scientific means. Muscle testing is a type of deductive reasoning and has been around for about a hundred years in one form or another.

Finally, muscle testing is not a tool for diagnosing illness. While it can be helpful to identify specific imbalances, blockages, reactions, and weaknesses, as well as identifying some helpful resolutions; it is not intended to be a diagnostic tool. You *can* use muscle testing as part of your decision-making process when evaluating a medical recommendation or treatment proposal, but not to do the diagnosing. Leave that to trained medical professionals and diagnosis tools.

In summary, with an appropriate mindset, muscle testing can be a wonderful tool to help you gain valuable information regarding your wellbeing. When abused or used inappropriately, muscle testing can be frustrating, cause additional difficulties, and even provide misinformation. So, always use this skill as it is intended—as a tool for self-discovery—and it will be a great benefit to you.

CHAPTER 5

Asking Good Questions

Asking good questions can be an art form when it comes to muscle testing and answering the mysteries of your life. At its simplest, muscle testing is a true/false method that starts with clear and specific yes/no questions. When you ask a question, the testing method you use will give you a yes or no answer. There are no long answers in muscle testing. You can apply it to work with multiple choice questions too, but in reality it's still just a series of yes/no questions.

When we begin using the muscle-testing methods, you will practice with very simple yes/no questions and true/false statements. These simple, clear questions will be about universal truths and things you know the answers to. They will give you an opportunity to practice without thinking too hard and introduce you to the process of asking questions and receiving answers.

Ask Clear Questions

While simple is a good place to start, clear will always be essential. You want to formulate every question with clarity. It matters what you ask and how you ask it. The clearer the question, the clearer and easier the answer is to understand.

Semantics can be an important consideration when asking questions, especially if you are aware of the nuances. I was working with a client who wanted to know if he could develop his muscle testing and coaching skills to help his family. He asked, "Can I use this work to help my family?"

While this may appear to be a good question, it is actually very vague. Now, this is someone I have worked with and trained for several years and is quite brilliant, and yet this tiny nuance short circuited his line of questioning. He tested *no* to this question. It didn't seem to make sense, so we analyzed his question.

First, saying *can* technically refers to *the ability* to do something. Only use *can* if that's what you really intend.

Second, he's already been helping his family for years but was feeling inadequate when it came to the very deep and difficult struggles they were having. The *no* answer he received reflected his present ability to help his family in those more challenging circumstances.

What he was actually asking was closer to his second, reworded question: "Is it right, according to my personal path and purpose, to develop these skills so I can help my family through any challenge?" To this very clear and specific question, he tested *yes*. This deep and meaningful question led to a profound shift in focus for this good father.

While I want to help you get to the deeper questions, it's best to start out much more simply. Focus on the simple things around you that you would like more information about. Ask questions like:

- Is it best for me to eat an apple right now?

- Do I need any supplements this morning?

- Does my body need more water today?

You can step it up a bit when you're ready and ask questions like:

- Is there a lesson I need to learn from my challenges?

- Is there an emotion underlying my discomfort?

- Am I being limited in my success by a negative belief about myself?

The point is to always keep your questions very clear. If your question is not clear, you may get a squishy answer or none at all. (*Squishy* is my favorite word to describe when muscle testing produces an unclear or half-hearted answer.)

Here are some examples of unclear questions.

- Is this food good for me?

Good for you how? Nutritionally? To give you energy? To help you lose weight? To not make you sick?

- Can I eat this food?

Well, can you? Are you physically able to eat this food? Are you missing teeth and wondering if it's possible to eat it?

Be clear about what you're really asking. Are you actually wanting to know if you will have a reaction to the food? Then, ask that.

- Is *xyz* supplement better for me?

Why might this question be unclear? Is xyz supplement better than what? Is it better than abc supplement? That could work.

Even clearer would be to ask if *xyz* supplement is better than *abc* supplement *right now*. Or you could ask if you need any right now at all.

- Should I drink more water?

Why is this unclear? Again, it's semantics. The word should is an external judgement. Should according to whom or what standard?

Does my body need more water today? is better because it asks whether more water would be beneficial to the body at that point in time. It could even be improved by asking: Would drinking 8 ounces of water be good for me right now? You could also increase or decrease the ounces and test again to identify the best amount for that moment.

You'll get used to asking these questions. And, you probably have dozens of questions already that you want answers to, which is very likely why you're reading this book. Just remember to pass your questions through the clarity filter first.

- Use a yes/no question or true/false statement.

- Make sure it's clear and precise so you will recognize the answer when you get it.
- Remember to keep it simple until you're confident with your testing.

Although it would be nice sometimes to just ask an open-ended question and get an answer, muscle testing doesn't work that way. As you hone your intuition, however, this type of open-ended questioning can provide remarkable information. We've seen some good examples of intuition and muscle testing working well together in previous chapters. For now, it's okay to stick with the guidelines above. You'll have a good foundation for muscle testing success.

Get Specific

Knowing which supplements and how much rest and proactive self-care our bodies are asking for can empower us to better care for our unique needs. Knowing what our bodies react to—in food, nature, chemicals, etc.—can make life much more comfortable, help us understand why our bodies respond the way they do, and keep us not only physically healthier but also mentally healthier.

This is most effective when we are specific with our questions. You can ask questions like:

- Am I having a reaction to the apple I ate?

- Do I need more Vitamin C in my diet?

- Is it best for me to exercise for 20 minutes today?

You can also ask deeper questions like:

- I feel resistance in moving toward my goal; do I need to understand something?

- Is my impatience adding to my stress today?

- Do I have any inherited patterns limiting my happiness?

This level of access to understanding ourselves and what can support our bodies' and minds' healing efforts is invaluable. Plus, when we are very clear and specific about what our question really is, we can more easily recognize the answer when we get it.

Here are some examples of non-specific versus specific questions:

Non-specific: Am I reacting to something I ate?
Specific: Am I having a reaction to the apple I ate?

The only value in asking the non-specific question here is if you think there may be several other factors that could cause the reaction you're experiencing. Then you can narrow down your questions further until you're asking very specific ones. If you just ate a casserole with several ingredients, you can start with the more general question and then test through specific items until you identify the culprit.

Non-specific: Am I getting all the nutrients I need in my diet?
Specific: Do I need more Vitamin C in my diet?

Again, a non-specific question like this could be a step into the conversation to identify why you're getting sick often or feel tired when you don't think you should, but by itself it's almost useless. Stepping into a more detailed set of questions will get you more helpful information that you can act on.

Non-specific: Is it good for me to exercise?
Specific: Is it best for me to exercise for 20 minutes today?

You can see where this is going, right? The more specific the question, the better the information you can gather. The non-specific question is probably a universal *yes* for everyone on the planet. It's not really a helpful question unless you're coming off of an illness or injury where it really isn't a good idea for you to exercise. Adding in the specifics of *best*, *20 minutes*, and *today* can help you navigate what your body really needs right now.

Sometimes you might not easily be able to start with a clear and specific question. You may need to start more broadly and ask narrowing questions as you go. Say you're experiencing a stomachache. There may not be an obvious cause for it, so you could ask a series of questions to get to the root of it.

The questioning could look like this:

- Is there something I need to know about my stomachache? *Yes.*

- Does my stomach hurt because of something I ate? *No.*

- Does it hurt because I'm getting sick? *No.*

- Does it hurt because I'm feeling anxious about something? *Yes.*

- Is it helpful to identify why I'm feeling anxious? *Yes.*

- Does it have something to do with my kids? *No.*

- Does it have something to do with work? *Yes.*

- Does it have to do with the new expectations on me at work? *Yes.*

- Is there anything else I need to know about why my stomach hurts? *Yes.*

- Is there a lesson I need to learn? *Yes.* Remember to give yourself space to listen for an answer. Possible lesson: *I need to trust my ability to do the job I was hired to do. I have strengths and the capacity to do great work.*

This drilling down exercise could just have easily followed the food route. Maybe you test strong, or *yes*, for food as the root cause of your stomachache. You could think about the last few things you ate and test through them. Or, you could test through food groups and then specific food items to narrow it down and discover the answer. Then identify the necessary change that needs to happen.

In the next chapter, we'll talk about how you can also draw from helpful resources to get more specific with your questions.

CHAPTER 6

Using Your Resources

In Chapter 2 we learned about the Journey Framework that I use for creating change with muscle testing:

1. **Face the Challenge**

2. **Learn the Lesson**

3. **Make the Change**

Frameworks such as this are crucial to helping us identify the truth nuggets we need from the endless stacks of information piled all around us. Then, in Chapter 5, we learned the importance of asking clear, specific questions so that we can access truth and get the answers we need.

In this chapter we will talk about how learning to identify resources to test through can be very helpful when seeking understanding about and working through our challenges.

Sifting through the seemingly endless options available to us can seem overwhelming. Conveniently, the logic is very similar to online shopping, something we have all become increasingly familiar with. Each shopping site has innumerable products to choose from, but they also provide the ability to set filters. With each filter we choose, the options narrow until we are able to find precisely what we're looking for.

Muscle testing through lists and other contained groupings plays a similar "filtering" role. These are among the more effective resources to guide our muscle testing and help us ask powerful questions as we seek answers for our needs.

A list can simply be defined as any grouping of options that you can muscle test through. Some lists are clearly defined, such as "the best 50 foods for women in their 40s" or "the top 20 books for entrepreneurs." Others are not presented as "lists" but provide categorized items to test through. This could include the photos in a style magazine to guide you in revamping your wardrobe or a display of paint swatches to help determine what wall color would provide the best environment for your family.

Whatever the source, look for lists or groupings that relate to your concern, ones that contain options you've been wondering about. If you're worried about environmental allergies, find a list online or in a book. If you're wondering about losing weight, find a list of strategies to test through to identify one that could be helpful for you. Maybe you're wanting to create a new family dinner menu. You could test through your favorite recipe books or apps.

If you can't find just the right list, make it. I've created several pages of things to test through from foods to emotions to body systems to environmental elements and more. This is a very important skill to learn, so I dedicate an entire chapter to creating your own lists later in this book. For now, use what you have on hand.

Easy sources to test through for common food concerns are the pantry or refrigerator. It's a good place to start identifying which foods are healthy, neutral, or causing reactions. If that's not complete enough, find a food list online or in a book.

If you have a collection of workout videos, you can muscle test through those one at a time to identify which would be most beneficial on a particular day.

If you're looking for resources to help you with mental or emotional concerns, you could find a list of emotions to test through. Emotions are funny, so a list like this can help you recognize more clearly what you're feeling or whether there are subtle, underlying emotions to a particular challenge. You could also account for people, places, and things that are in your environment on a regular basis to identify triggers that you may be reacting to.

If you are moving toward a goal, you could test through your bookshelf of personal development books for the best one to read right now or for individual concepts you need to review or grow in. You could also test through a list of books online to find the next one to buy.

I have used muscle testing to test through which makeup products would be best for my skin and which soaps would be best for my family. I have even tested through a list of movies to help determine which one would be most enjoyable or beneficial for my family to watch together. Testing through kids' lunch snacks at the grocery store or sore throat drops at the pharmacy is a common occurrence.

(Quick note: At the risk of being repetitive, you can absolutely use this skill to seek the wellbeing of others, particularly your family. It's not only ok to ask about how you can bless your loved ones, it's great! We'll talk more about how to do this in a later chapter.)

Some of my favorite sources to test through early on were books created about essential oils and flower essences. The authors were really insightful folks who offered deeper meanings into these natural resources. They helped me learn some profound things about myself and understand why I was experiencing certain difficulties.

It wasn't always the words they used; it was often the thoughts they prompted that gave them meaning to me. I pondered the line or words in the description of the oil or essence that I tested for to understand what dots it was connecting. You can use this process through any number of resources that are meaningful to you.

It's important to remember that muscle testing doesn't do the thinking for you; it helps you tap into the information inside of you to know what is good for you. So do your homework. As you go through these resources, learn what you can about them. Read the descriptions and reviews to understand what you're getting (or getting yourself into). Muscle testing can speed up the process, but it does not replace our responsibility to think our own thoughts and make our own choices.

Also, remember to always have the best intentions—to understand what's best for your personal wellbeing. Keep your biases clear. Be open to truths that may be unexpected or disappointing, too. The lists you use are only as good as your connection to the knowledge inside of you.

One of the best ways to ensure you're in the right mindset is to stay grounded about what you want to learn and remain connected to the greater good. If you need to meditate or pray to keep clear and focused, then by all means, do that! Do whatever helps you open to and connect with truth, and do it often. It will make all the difference.

When we use the resources we have around us, we can more easily access helpful guidance to understanding our challenges, learn the lessons they have for us, and even begin making valuable changes in our lives. This wonderful knowledge is readily available to us with the skill of muscle testing, so let's get into the various methods of how to do it.

PART 2

"Often, it's not about becoming a new person, but becoming the person you were meant to be, and already are, but don't know how to be."

~ Heath L. Buckmaster

CHAPTER 7

Self-Muscle Testing Methods

This chapter is where the rubber hits the road. Up to this point, you've been learning much of the backstory and underlying principles of how muscle testing works. Now, it's time to introduce you to several of the common muscle testing methods. You don't have to master them all. The goal is to find which way or ways work most reliably for you so you can have success.

The goal is to become self-sufficient in muscle testing, so this chapter focuses on techniques you can do yourself—aka self-muscle testing. In the next chapter, we'll touch on how you can use some of these methods with other people.

There are many methods of muscle testing—countless, even. In this chapter we will learn seven of the more common techniques, ranging from using the whole body to just a couple of fingers. As you try each one, see which works best for you. Like anything else, it takes practice to become really comfortable and proficient at self-muscle testing, so be patient and just do your best.

What you're looking for as you experiment with these methods are the ones where you sense the change in balance or strength. You may find that the larger movements are easier for you. Or, you may find that you're sensitive to smaller movements and enjoy the subtler methods.

To get the most out of this instruction, take the time to work through each method and discover which one works best for you. You're the only one who can learn it for you.

SWAY

The Sway method uses the whole body. It can be easier than the other methods, as the movements are larger and more noticeable. When asking a question, you will sense the answer as your body moves either forward or backward.

This method is done in a standing position. As you refine your sense for the movement, you may also be able to use the Sway method effectively while seated or kneeling if standing is not possible or practical in the moment. The key is being able to sense clearly the forward or backward motion of your body.

When getting ready to use the Sway test, make sure you are standing straight and tall. Get your balance. You may find it easier to sense the shift in balance with your shoes off.

Your intention will help you calibrate your body to respond clearly to your questions. Tell your body that falling slightly forward means that the answer to your question is *yes* or that it is *true*. This also means that falling slightly backward means that the answer to your question is *no* or that it is *false*.

Give it a try. Make sure you're standing nice and tall. Start with a question that has a universally positive answer so you can focus on how it feels rather than whether or not it's true.

Ask yourself the question: Is water good for me? Wait a moment for your body to respond. Is it falling forward? You can also use a statement such as: My name is ... (fill in your name). Then wait for your body to respond.

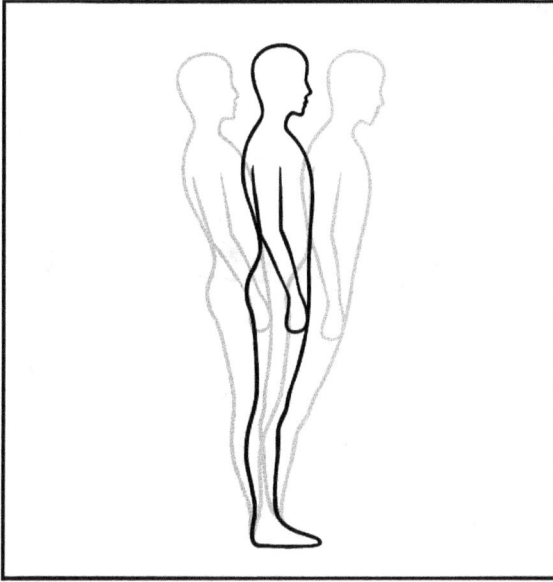

It should fall forward to confirm that what you said is true. Keep trying until you feel the sensation one way or the other, and repeat it until the feeling becomes familiar and natural.

FOREARM LEVER

The Forearm Lever method is another larger-type movement method. It requires you to distinguish between force and resistance instead of the Sway method's sensation of falling forward or backward. The forearm acts as the body in the Sway method. The fingers of the opposite hand act as the testing force.

To use this method, you may stand up or sit down. Keep a good posture with your shoulders square. Apply gentle downward pressure on your forearm with your fingers. It isn't really about muscling; it's about perceiving the answer that arises inside us through the external physical interaction between pressing and resisting. The information flows through us and out to our muscles and limbs where we can more easily see and feel its effects, thus recognizing an answer.

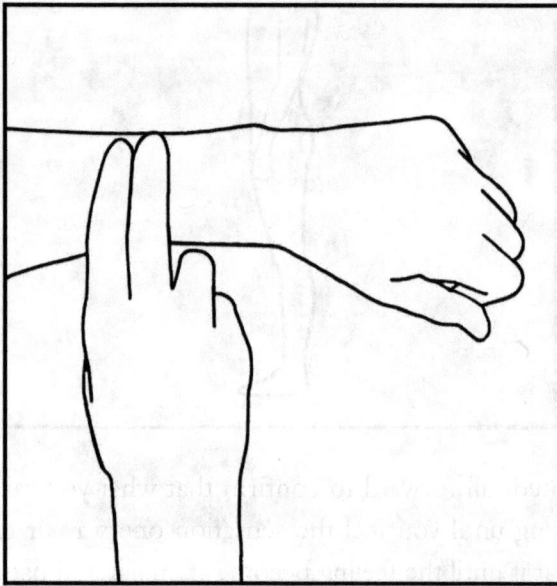

Set the intention that a *yes* or *true* response shows up as strength in your forearm and clear resistance to the downward pressure of your fingers. Conversely, a *no* or *false* answer will move your forearm easily.

Ask yourself a question or make a statement that you know to be affirmative. You may state your eye or hair color. You could reference being inside or outside. How is it working?

Now try a question that you know to be negative right now. Ask: Is it good for me to eat sugar all day?

Obviously the answer is *no* and your arm should go down. Experiment further to see how your body responds to this method.

PLIERS

The Pliers method is a more subtle movement. As with the Forearm Lever method, people typically use their non-dominant hand as the indicator and the dominant hand as the testing force, but you can choose which hand will exert the pressure and which hand will receive it.

As you see in the pictures, make a circle with the fingers of your left hand (if you're right-handed). It can be your thumb with the finger that's most comfortable. I usually use my middle finger here. With your right hand, bring the tips of your thumb, forefinger, and middle finger together. These act as pliers, in a way, applying outward force to the connected fingers of the left hand.

Try it out by making the circle with your non-dominant hand and the pliers position with the three fingers of your dominant hand. Place the pliers into the circle of the opposite hand.

When you ask your question, a *yes* answer is the circle staying closed while the pliers attempt to softly pry them open. A *no* answer is the pliers easily opening the circle of the other hand. Give this one a try.

Ask something like: Is it best for me to eat an apple today? or Do I need more protein in my diet?

Remember, with the *yes* answer, the circle stays closed and the *no* answer opens the circle.

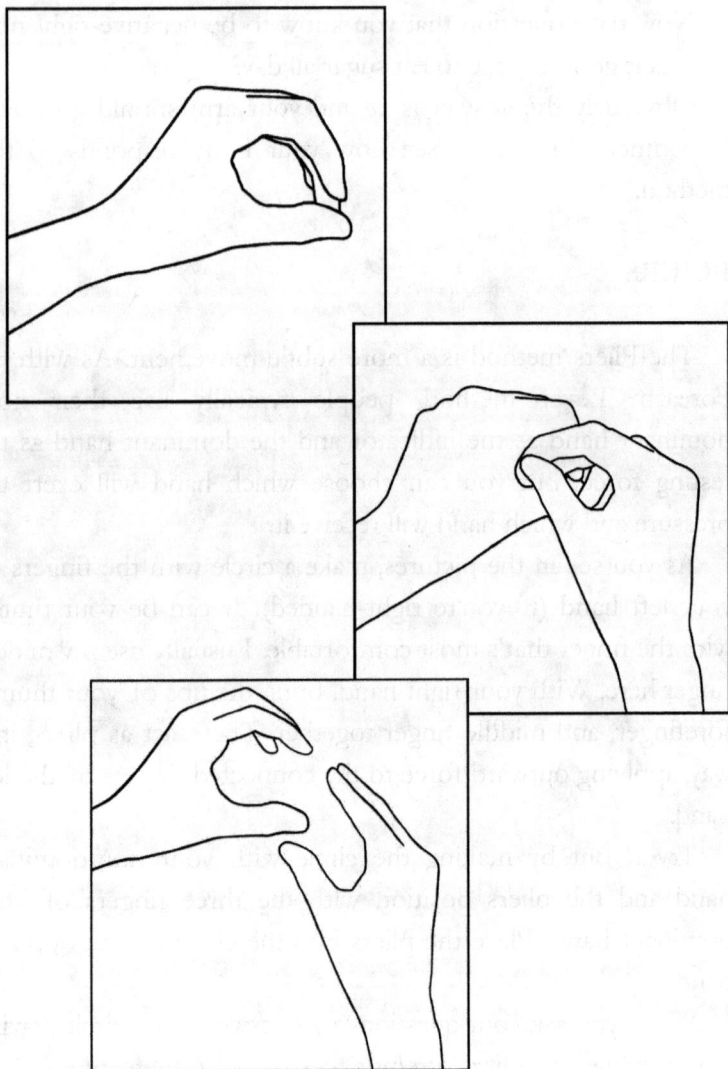

Don't think too hard about this or assume you know the answer. A bias such as this can influence the testing and give you an inaccurate answer.

RINGS

The Rings method is very similar to the Pliers method, but with the hands making two circles. The circle of your non-dominant hand will give the answer (it will open or stay closed) as the circle on the dominant hand stays closed throughout the test.

Try this one and see if you can sense the strength or weakness, the *yes* or *no*. Ask another *yes* or *no* question or make a *true* or *false* statement to test. Then, pull your hands away from each other and try to open the ring.

You could ask about exercise: Is it best for me to go for a walk today? Insert whatever your favorite (or least offensive) exercise is there. You could also ask if it's best to exercise for more than 15 minutes? or 30 minutes?

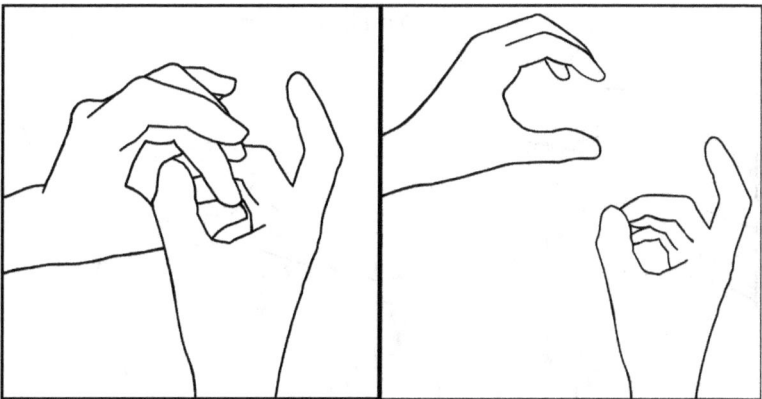

Practice keeping your non-dominant hand relaxed and responsive to the information coming through it. This hand is the gate to all the answers you need.

Also remember to keep your dominant hand locked in and steady. Let it be the constant that you set in place and don't worry about. When it's well set, you can focus your mind more easily on sensing the answers in the non-dominant hand.

FINGER-IN-RING

The Finger-in-Ring method is another variation on the base ring position. It works much like the Rings method of pulling your finger circles apart trying to see if the non-dominant hand opens.

This method simply uses the ring on one hand and the forefinger of the other. You move the straight finger toward the fingertips of the ring for the *yes* or *no* answer. If the ring stays closed at the fingertips, the answer is *yes*. If the finger breaks through the fingertips, the answer is *no*.

Try this method, but be kind to your forefinger. Keep it strong as it moves to open the ring and remember that you don't have to push too hard. You don't want to strain it.

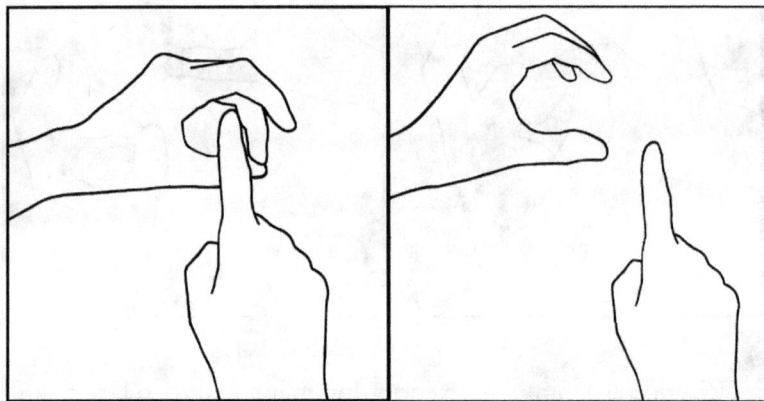

Try asking a question about some personal development this time.

For example, ask if you have a book in your personal library that can help you move toward your goals. Or, ask if it would be best to watch an inspirational video someone suggested recently. Take a moment to ask a meaningful question that can move you forward somehow.

If you're still working to get the feel of muscle testing and want a simpler question, try asking a question about your emotional state: Am I peaceful? or Am I stressed about something?

You could also make statements and test for *true* or *false* answers: I am hungry, or I am willing to learn. Or even, I feel confident.

Whatever the question or statement, keep it clear and meaningful to you. If what you're asking doesn't feel relevant, your body may resist answering the question.

FRICTION

The Friction method is pictured here in three ways. You can apply it with just about any surface that has at least some friction. The idea is that the closing or resisting energy that illustrates a *yes* or *true* answer through strength can be applied to a side-to-side, or back-and-forth, movement here.

In the first image, you are sliding the pads of your thumb and a finger across each other. The *yes* answer has more friction and is more difficult to slide. The *no* answer has less friction and is easier to slide.

The second image shows moving the pad of your finger across the opposite forearm to gauge friction.

The third image is sliding your finger across a piece of paper, the surface of a desk, or any other handy surface.

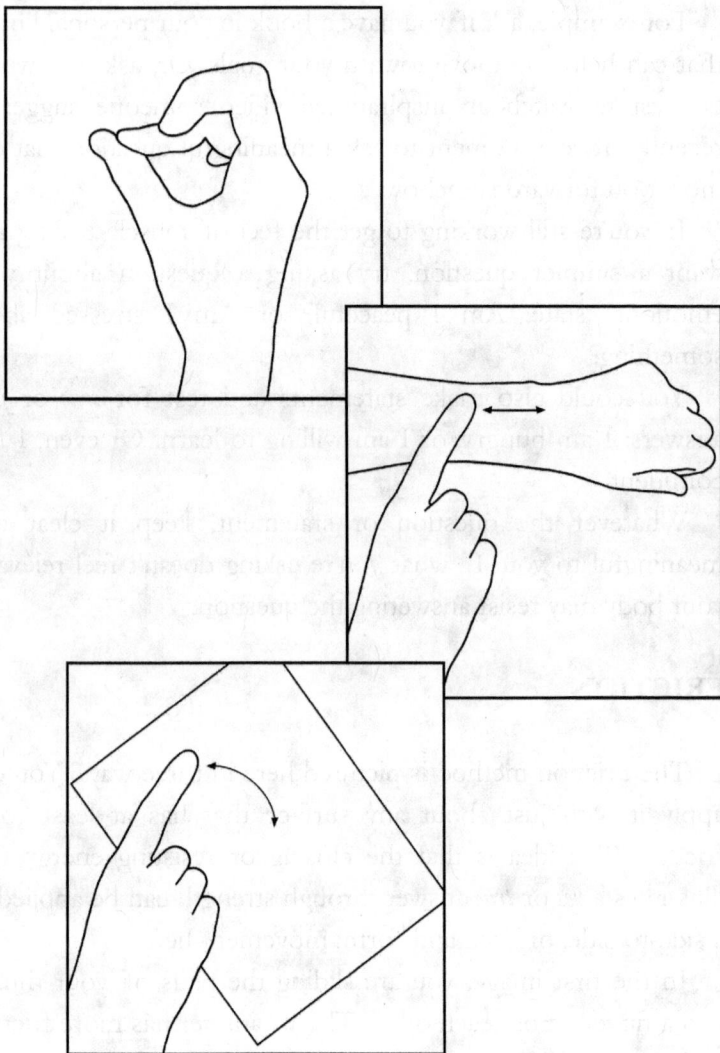

Give this one a try to see if you can sense the difference in levels of friction with your fingertips.

**The most important thing right now is to keep working on developing your muscle-testing skills. However, if you are feeling good about your progress or a bit adventurous, you may consider asking a more advanced question, such as: Is there something I need to know about the pain I keep feeling in my neck or back or feet, etc.?

Whatever question you're up for, give it a try now.

****

Before I share the last method, remember that these are only a few common methods of muscle testing. In reality, there are dozens of ways to apply this skill.

If you tend to be very aware of subtle shifts in your body, for example, you may be able to use that as your indicator. Sensations such as a muscle tightening in your neck, a flutter in your eyelids, a warmth in your chest, or a peaceful feeling can all work. The sky's the limit. It all depends upon your level of sensitivity and your intention.

RING

The final technique is also my favorite—the Ring method. It relies on you being very sensitive to the feeling between your fingers.

When you use the Pliers or other Rings methods, you may notice a magnetic-like sensation between your fingertips when you test positive to your questions. This *yes* answer creates a strength in the connection between your fingers that can be sensed without the use of a second hand initiating the test. You can simply use the muscles in the back of your Ring hand to pull the fingers apart.

The *yes* test feels like your fingers won't let go, almost like there is a magnet holding them together. The *no* test simply allows the ring to open easily. If this feels too advanced, don't worry. Just review and work through the other methods to find the one that is comfortable for you right now and work up to this one if you want.

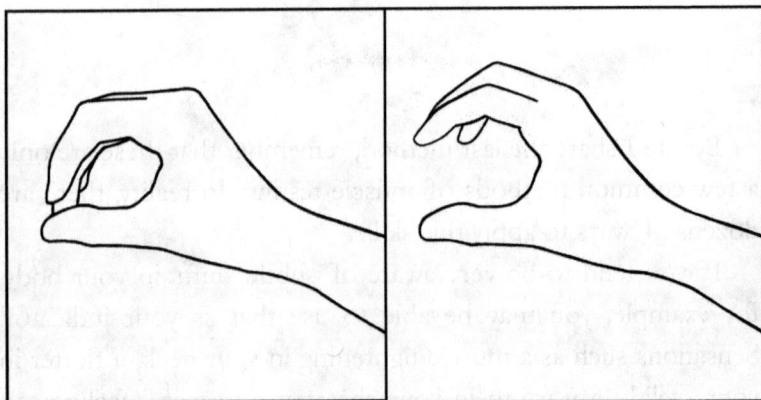

I like this method because it is very subtle, and it allows me to be more attentive while I'm testing. Also, I can test for hours at a time with this method without getting tired or sore. When I'm coaching someone and they need a lot of testing done for them, I can easily stay focused and the session can go as long as it needs to.

Give this method a quick try. It may be exactly how your body wants to communicate with you.

Ask yourself another simple question, or maybe something deeper. Make the statement: I am fully committed to doing what it takes to improve the quality of my life, or I am all in to reaching my goal. How do they test? Are you all in?

If you didn't test strong for being completely committed to moving forward in your life, I invite you to consider why not and make the decision now to get there.

****

These are just a few of the many methods for self-muscle testing. Hopefully you have found one that feels good to you. If not, research and experiment with additional options until you find the method that works best for you.

Muscle testing alone can be a bit tricky as you're getting started. In the next chapter, we will explore how to use muscle testing with someone else. Working with another person as you begin learning can let you focus on fewer factors in the muscle-testing process. Practicing with another person can help you build confidence in your new skill. And, you will be helping someone learn this valuable new tool.

CHAPTER 8

Muscle Testing with Others

While I learned the basics for muscle testing on my own, I refined my skill by working with my husband. Learning together helped both of us become more confident to move forward with the self-testing methods.

Not only could we help each other improve our abilities to test, we also helped each other find better questions to ask. We helped each other discover wonderful answers that moved us forward toward our personal and professional goals. So, if you can find someone willing to go on this journey with you, it could make your experience that much better!

In this chapter, we will cover two ways to muscle test with another person. The first one adapts the Forearm Lever method. The second one uses the base ring position.

First, consider the Forearm Lever method. One person can use their arm and be the tested side while the second person can use their hand to press down on the first person's arm. It can be localized to the forearm or the first person can stretch their full arm out to their side or in front of them. The second person then presses down on the extended forearm to test regarding a question.

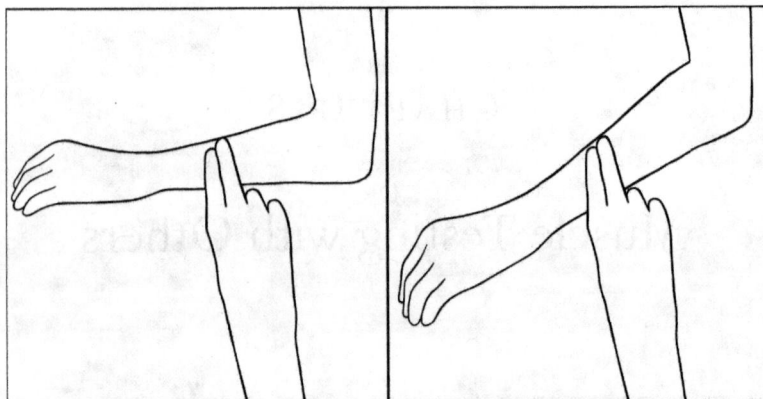

As you can see, this limits the focus for each person to only paying attention to one aspect of the muscle-testing process. It can help build confidence one piece at a time. This can also help with avoiding bias when testing through questions that may carry strong opinions.

The Rings method is another common way to muscle test with two people. The first person makes a ring with their fingers. The second person uses two hands to pull the first person's fingers open.

Each person focuses on their particular task, ensuring they use mild effort. Remember, we're not using a lot of strength in either role. The intention is to discern the answers to our questions through subtle shifts in strength. Just relax and allow the answers to surface.

Take turns with both you and your muscle-testing partner performing each role. Get used to how little strength is needed to discover your answers on each side. This type of practice can help build your confidence with self-muscle testing.

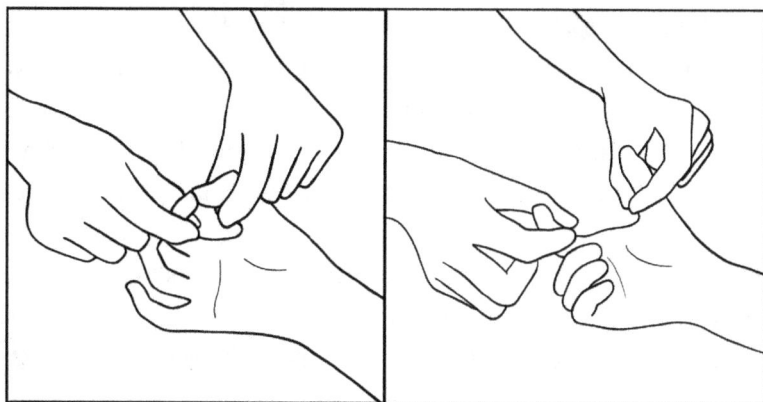

Early in our muscle-testing journey, my husband and I often used this version of the Rings method together. While we had dabbled in the solo methods, we felt a lot more comfortable practicing with each other, especially when there were a lot of questions we wanted to ask.

One afternoon, we were visiting my husband's parents at their home. At one point, we were muscle testing together to identify some contributing factors to a concern he had. He made the ring with his fingers, and I exerted gentle force to try to open the ring with each question. Since we were sitting at the kitchen table, I was asking questions in a quiet tone.

I asked a few questions and tested through each one. He was half-paying attention to his parents' conversation while I was testing on his hand, and I was in my own world focusing on the questions as his fingers gave the answers. I guess at some point I stopped asking the questions out loud, but kept testing with his hand.

After a minute or two, he looked at me grinning and said, "Hey, it's pretty cool that you can use telepathy to do this." I stopped, eyes wide and thought, *Wait, what!?*

Now, I know that's not exactly what was happening, but it gave me pause for a moment. Then, it occurred to me that the energetic network of communication that always allowed me to ask questions inside of myself had also allowed me to ask my husband's body questions and get answers. Amazing!

From there, I tried it out intentionally and it worked every time. My intentions to ask questions for his wellbeing were able to communicate with the universal energetic network that connects us all. This inspired me to ask if I could muscle test for our children. *Yep. I sure could.*

This powerful truth has been life changing. I began testing for how I could help my children better, to understand their needs, and to help them heal from their illnesses and difficulties more effectively.

I asked additional questions after that. I wanted to know if I could muscle test for others I was helping and for family members in other states. I tested *yes!* This was incredible to me, and I started practicing right away. Now, I don't think twice about it.

As I continued exploring the possibilities here, I learned that we need permission to test for other people. Once we have permission, your intention can usually tap into the information flowing through them. Our young children are an exception; we can test for them anytime.

As you become more confident with your muscle-testing skills, try giving a friend a call in another city or state and ask if you can practice with them. Start by asking about things that they can confirm. You'll want to know that you can sustain accurate testing in a new context.

Not only can muscle testing with another person help you build your confidence, the act of explaining the process to them will help ingrain the principles more deeply into your own mind. By teaching it, you will understand it better and, in turn, improve your muscle-testing skills overall.

As with anything, the best way to develop this new skill is to practice. In the next chapter, we'll delve into practicing what you've learned so you can explore what this skill can really do for you. I love the quote by Ludwig van Beethoven, "Don't only practice your art, but force your way into its secrets; art deserves that, for it and knowledge can raise man to the Divine." So, whether you're looking for inspiration or just some simple answers, you can discover the beauty deep inside of you that's waiting to shine.

CHAPTER 9

Practice

Now that you have been introduced to the various muscle-testing methods, it's time to practice. Practice asking about different foods, supplements, exercise habits, emotions you're feeling, and more. Jump in and learn about how to improve your wellbeing.

Since you understand how muscle testing works, experiment with each of these methods until you find the one that feels most natural to you. Some will work, but feel awkward. With others, you may not feel answers at all. There's nothing wrong with you. Just keep going until one speaks to you. Even if it takes a while, one will likely rise above the rest to be your go-to method. Just keep practicing until you feel confident.

Here are a few tips and reminders to help you refine your new skill.

1. **Manage your biases.** Once you've determined which method you want to work with, build your confidence by practicing with simple positive and negative answers. Work to get so familiar with the process of muscle testing and managing your biases that it becomes second nature to trust your answers.

2. **Use small amounts of pressure.** In each of these methods, we're applying the smallest levels of effort possible to see results. It's a matter of allowing these energetic messages to flow through you and surface in a way that you can recognize clearly and consistently.

3. **Trust the process and believe in yourself.** If you're feeling doubtful because you don't understand how it all works or are struggling to believe that you can do it, relax, breathe, and trust that you know enough to get started. Muscle testing will eventually become so familiar that you won't think about how it works; you will just know that it does.

4. **Keeping your intention focused.** Intention is a key element to effective muscle testing. When you practice, choose to believe that you have access to the answers that you need and that you will recognize them when they come.

5. **Commit to daily practice.** Set a time each day to build your skill. Work at testing consistently for at least the next four weeks. Build the habit of being in tune with and identifying what your body needs and what is best for it.

6. **Increase your sensitivity.** Pay attention to the sensations while you test so that you can become more aware of them. It may be difficult at first to discern the balance or strength or weakness, but it will come. Over time, you can develop the necessary sensitivity to test easily and accurately.

7. **Review the basics.** If muscle testing isn't coming quickly to you after going through this book once, go through it again.

Go back and practice again and again to become more familiar with the movements and sensations, and asking good questions. Remember that it may also be helpful to practice with another person.

8. Be kind and be patient with yourself. A quiet heart learns better than an anxious one. This is a skill you may need to work to develop. You are just fine if it doesn't come at once. But it will come. Keep going and remind yourself that this is a skill worth the effort.

9. Set short-term goals. I invite you to set a goal to learn to test well within the next few weeks. Determine your go-to method for testing, and commit to practicing a few minutes each day.

10. Have reasonable expectations. Your expectations will create your experience. Take a quick accounting of your expectations for yourself, especially if you find yourself becoming impatient. Holding unreasonable expectations is a great way to sabotage yourself, so give yourself time and space to breathe while your skills develop.

A lovely lady I know has tried to learn muscle testing for years, but it never really locked into place for her. She would get it working for a short time, and then it would seem to short circuit. But she never gave up.

Recently, I shared this new muscle-testing training with her, and it finally became clear. She had that *Aha* moment and everything just clicked into place. She can test confidently and clearly now. It took her a bit longer than she wanted, but she persisted and succeeded.

As you build your confidence with muscle testing, you will find that it offers so many benefits for your life. It's a great tool to help you *face your challenges* and identify elements contributing to them. It can help you filter through thoughts to *learn the lessons* your trials are trying to teach you. It can also help lead you to *make real change* in your life as you lean into it.

With muscle testing, you can engage in the *alchemy of becoming* more intentionally and effectively. You can help the process of changing and improving your life to be inspiring and motivating. You can feel more and more empowered. In this process, you can create more peace, more joy, and more success. It's all at your fingertips!

CHAPTER 10

Troubleshooting

There may be times when your muscle testing seems to give you odd or squishy answers. You may feel confused, like something about the answer is off, or maybe your testing method is malfunctioning. It is important to always keep your testing reliable, so here are some tips for troubleshooting.

First, double check that your question or statement is clear, simple, and specific. Be sure you know what you're asking so you will clearly recognize the answer.

Have you ever seen the movie *IQ*? I love the line that Albert Einstein (played by Walter Matthau) says to the young garage mechanic/aspiring scientist Ed Walters (played by Tim Robbins) as they're going for a walk.

Einstein tells Walters about having a triple scoop ice cream cone when he first arrived in the US. Walters asks Einstein, "What flavor?" Einstein responds, "Peppermint."

Then he adds: "You see, this is a good question. 'What flavor?' Simple, specific, and it has an answer."

Second, clearer answers come when you are unbiased and unattached to the outcome. Remember to always desire to know the truth and keep yourself neutral on the result of the test. Any opinions or assumptions about the answer to your question can influence the test. You can't learn what you need when you're blocked to possible outcomes or you assume you know the answer.

Always set the intention to access truths that will help you improve your personal wellbeing and move you forward in your life. Then, be open to the truths that come, even ones that may be difficult to hear, such as: get more sleep, go to bed earlier, entertain positive instead of negative thoughts, be more generous with your time toward your family, be kind to that grumpy co-worker, or be brave about reaching for your dreams. It has been said that truth makes us free. It is very much the case here.

If you find yourself really wanting a specific answer, it will make it very difficult to get a truly clear answer. Why are you asking the question in the first place? You want to know what's best for you, don't you? Then, you have to put yourself in a space to receive what is best, not just validate what you want. Calm any fear or ego and quiet any predetermined opinions that may interfere.

One day I was helping a client uncover a series of limiting paradigms that were preventing her from being successful in her business endeavors. She actually had several opportunities she was juggling and couldn't understand why none of them were meeting her expectations for success.

As we talked through each of them, we tested to identify how good for her and her family each opportunity rated. What we found was surprising. The one that she was the most resistant to tested the strongest for her.

She struggled with the results of our testing, so we asked more questions. We discovered that there were several layers of limiting beliefs, disinterest, and discouragement surrounding this neglected business opportunity. These blocks and paradigms of internal resistance had been causing the lack of success in this area of her life.

It took a few more questions and some effort to resolve each of these blocks, but she began to feel the resistance dissipate. We continued to identify and work through each layer that caused her to neglect this business until she started to see the possibilities in it. We kept going until she was actually excited about moving that business forward.

By using muscle testing to identify the reasons behind this business opportunity's lack of success and what needed to be resolved within her so she could fully embrace it, she was able to see its potential and begin making a plan for its revival. Sometimes it's difficult to see what is best for us when it's buried deep inside.

Removing your bias may take practice, but it is essential to accurate testing.

Third, calm is key. When muscle testing, you may be more effective the closer you can get to something of a meditative state. I don't mean that you need to start levitating in that classic meditative position, but the calm, focused, open, and relaxed space of meditation is perfect for asking clear, specific questions and sensing the answers.

In this space you can quietly think about your questions and even say them aloud if it helps you to focus. This calm state can help keep your testing reliable.

If you're feeling angry, frustrated, overwhelmed, stubborn, panicked, or shocked, your muscle testing will likely be compromised. When you're in this kind of state, do what you can to calm yourself, or wait for a better time so that you can test accurately. You may get confused and frustrated trying to force a test in this state.

I have felt short-circuited by these kinds of feelings many times, especially when one of my kids was really upset about something. Whether it appeared to be physical pain or emotional turmoil, I would be anxious to find a quick solution. So, I would start testing through ideas that came to mind but found that I felt confused, and it showed in my testing.

I wouldn't be able to sense clearly whether I was testing *yes* or *no* for the thoughts I was asking about. I'd keep trying, but would continue to get squishy answers. This made me feel even more anxious, impatient, and worried.

When my husband was available, I'd ask him to help me test through some of my ideas to determine if any of them were right and if he could think of anything else. When he wasn't close by and it was all up to me, I learned that I needed to calm myself down for my testing to work again.

In that situation, I would say a quick prayer and focus my intention on getting myself into a space where I could think and test clearly. Only then was I able to test accurately and receive helpful answers.

Through much practice and frustration, I have learned where to start when I'm faced with stressful situations. I hope these thoughts help you as well.

Fourth, remember to use muscle testing how it's designed— to help you improve your wellbeing. If you try to use it for mind reading, fortune telling, or some other questionable intention, it will short circuit.

Sometimes you may not be sure whether your question is okay to ask. This is actually a great awareness. Whenever I come across a situation like this, I back up and simply ask, "Is it okay to ask this question?" If I test *no*, I reconsider what I'm really wanting to know. Then, I try to reword the question to get the information I need. And sometimes I realize that what

I'm seeking crosses the line of what is appropriate for muscle testing, so I stop and work to get back on the right track.

Fifth, you may need to release some interference. There may be a belief making it difficult for you to be completely unbiased or an emotion preventing you from testing clearly. In just a few chapters, I will share with you a technique that can help you to resolve the interference. Stay tuned!

On a final note, there are a lot of opinions about what can interfere with proper muscle testing. Most of them are different ways of talking about the same problems I've already mentioned. Or they may be what people have come to believe are obstacles when, in fact, they are not. Beliefs hold powerful sway on our perceptions.

Many people talk about hydration as a key element to keeping your muscle testing reliably on. That's never been an issue for me, but it may be for someone else. If they believe muscle testing is more about electricity than energetic information, then the hydration issue could make sense, as it helps with conductivity. Understanding the energy side of the conversation, however, water becomes irrelevant.

Know this, if you follow the guidelines I've illustrated here —learning the skill, asking proper questions, keeping your biases and expectations in check, staying calm and clear, and resolving interference—you will be able to muscle test accurately whenever you desire. This approach has worked very well for me, my clients, and my students for several years.

Now that you've learned the methods of muscle testing and how to manage effective testing, let's take another step toward mastering the whole process and making real changes. That's what the next section is all about, starting with how to ask even better questions to get better answers.

PART 3

"Fall in love with the process of becoming the best version of yourself."

~ Anonymous

CHAPTER 11

Asking Better Questions

Asking good questions is an art form. As a coach I have asked thousands of questions over the years and have found solutions for some of the most difficult situations and health mysteries. It has taken great effort and patience to learn what to ask and when.

Good questions come from a sincere desire to know the truth, humility to receive the answer—whatever it may be—and a willingness to act on that truth to improve the quality of your life or the lives of those you care about.

You may need to get creative with your questions as you seek to understand the truths behind the challenge you're facing. Follow the Journey Framework I shared with you as you ask questions about your challenge. To review, they are:

Face the Challenge - Know what you're dealing with. Test through resources to identify factors that contribute to your issue.

Learn the Lesson - Learn what the challenge is trying to teach you. Evaluate the factors to understand what it all means to you.

Make the Change - Do what is necessary to move forward. Shift a behavior or environment or resolve an internal obstacle in order to overcome the challenge.

Over the years, my husband has been a wonderful guinea pig for everything I learn and want to experiment with. He is a golfer, and one day he was experiencing tightness in his muscles that was causing problems in his golf game. Here are the questions we used to walk through his challenge.

Face the Challenge

- Is there something I need to know about the tightness in my muscles? *Yes.*

- Is what I need to know on any testing pages? *No.* Since it was a no, he considered current events in his life, society, etc. *What came to mind was a feeling.*

- Is there an emotion contributing to the tightness? *Yes.* He thought for a moment and realized the feeling was *pessimism.*

- Is there another emotion? *Yes. Despair came to mind.*

- Is there a lesson in my muscle tightness? *Yes.* He listened for it and tested through thoughts that came to mind to see if they were relevant. He thought about his life priority list that he had previously prepared and tested through it for golf. (Yes, golf is on his priority list, and I completely support it.)

- Does golf have anything to do with pessimism or despair? *Yes, despair.*

- What does that mean to me? He thought for a moment.

- Am I feeling any despair about golf? *Yes.* He thought about that a bit and realized that he had a *limiting belief: "I will never be able to reach my potential."*

- Does the muscle tightness cause me to feel that way? *Yes, but it's more than that. He felt like his skills were deteriorating except for one perfect swing he'd had recently.*

- Can we isolate what's happening to limit the other swings? *Yes. He felt a catch in them.*

- Is there a particular factor we need to identify about the catch in the other swings? Is there something we can or need to know about it? *Yes.* It had to do with his *purpose.*

- Is there more we need to know there? *No.*

Learn the Lesson

- Is there a lesson or a message I need to understand? *Yes.* The thought came to him: *I know that this is an important part of my purpose. I need to trust the process and stop doubting and looking at all the obstacles.*

Make the Change

- Is there a change that needs to be made? *Yes.*

- Is it external / behavioral? *No.*

- Does something internal need to be resolved? *Yes.*

He focused his intention to remove the obstacle(s). (We used the techniques from my book *Life Above the Line*.)

- Is there anything else to resolve? *No.*

- Is there anything else I need to know, learn, or change about this tightness? *No.*

He determined that he would pay attention the next time he goes to swing to notice any difference. He also thought through the message to understand it more fully and let it sink in to facilitate the change. He consciously chose to receive the message and move forward.

RESULT - The next time he practiced at the course, it went better. There were noticeable improvements across the board. He was also able to recognize important elements of his technique that he could improve.

This is just one example of hundreds over the years where muscle testing has been incredibly helpful in learning valuable insights and overcoming challenges.

Even if all you do to start muscle testing is to learn important factors contributing to your challenges, this skill will begin to change your life.

What I wish for you is to go beyond that. Take the techniques that I will teach you in the next chapter, use the Journey Framework to guide your efforts, and make real, significant internal changes along with the necessary external ones.

This work can help you reach your goals, too! Just be clear and patient, and ask questions like a detective. Let muscle testing help you understand how you truly think and feel about your challenge and help you become more aware of your reactive behaviors that may be sabotaging your efforts to achieve your goals.

Muscle testing creates a powerful self-awareness that can arm you with information that is key to changing your life. The questions you ask put this process into motion.

Rating Your Pain

By establishing a standard—such as a scale from 0-10—we can use muscle testing to evaluate and rate our options. We can also rate the intensity of the challenges we face.

One example of using muscle testing to rate intensities came from a conversation I had with another student. She was working to overcome some bumps in her relationship with her husband. She wanted their relationship to be more peaceful and trusting, but things kept happening to sabotage her desires.

On one particular call, she told me how frustrated she was with him. Typically, when someone vents about another person, their voice grows intense, whereas they remain calm and reasonable when talking about themselves. This recounting, however, was completely the reverse.

She complained in a tense voice how irritated she felt about a recent situation involving her husband. Then, in a very soothing tone, she described to me how calm he was during it. Returning to the agitated tone, she explained how grumpy she was with something he had done, but that he was being very patient. With each grievance, she illustrated herself as antagonistic and him as kind; she was making herself sound unreasonable and him sound level-headed.

I smiled and said to her, "You're doing a really poor job of telling me how terrible he is with that sweet tone of voice." My comment stunned her for a moment, then she started laughing. She had been completely unaware of what she was doing. We both got a good chuckle out of it.

As we analyzed her tone, it became clear that her subconscious mind was sending her conflicting messages. One subconscious program was expressing her love for him, while a second, conflicting program was determined to justify her irritation with him.

As we tested through the elements contributing to her short circuit, we identified some of the opposing subconscious programs that were driving her curious behavior that day.

(Again, I've been doing this for a long time and can pretty easily identify beliefs, programs, and patterns that work against us. I also have additional frameworks supporting this effort that are beyond the scope of this book. But, you can still engage in the process for yourself, listen to your impressions, and begin having success now.)

With each program we identified, we rated how strongly they were influencing her behavior. It was very enlightening to see how some of these underlying beliefs were undermining her desire to build their relationship.

Once we identified and rated all the programs sabotaging her that day with her husband, we used the *Life Above the Line* techniques to strengthen the positive ones and remove the negative ones—the blocks—that were weakening them.

The extent of the work we did to shift things internally for my client is more than we will discuss in this book. But, I am sharing it with you here so you can begin to see how many doors can open and opportunities for healing and change are available when you become competent in the skill of muscle testing.

Practice

Let's practice rating things on a scale of 0-10. I'm going to ask you some questions that can act as a kind of self-assessment to help you gain some basic insights into your subconscious. The goal is to identify, on a scale of 0-10, how strong or true each statement is for you right now.

I find that it's easiest to ask if the strength is between 5 and 10 first. If yes, then ask about each number from 5-10 individually until you get a *yes*. 5? 6? 7? and so on. If you get a *no* to the 5-10 range, then test through the lower numbers: 4? 3? 2? etc., until you identify the number with a strong test.

Remember, the answers you get are only snapshots into your subconscious at this moment in time. The great news is that you can improve the quality of the information in your subconscious mind, so don't read too much into it. It's only information.

Ok, muscle test through the following statements to see how your subconscious perceives each one:

* I am valuable. (How strongly does your subconscious believe this statement? 0-10?)

- I have a strong influence over my life. (How strong does it test? 0-10?)

- I am resilient. (How strong is this for you? 0-10?)

- I have purpose. (How strong? 0-10?)

How did you do? Did you get any squishy answers? You may want to review the previous chapter and troubleshoot your muscle testing if something seems off.

If your testing was clear, what do you think about the answers? Were they validating of what you thought they would be? Or were there any surprises?

If they all tested strong, that's wonderful! I hope it is validating and encouraging. If they weren't as strong as you thought they should be, think about why they might be where they are. You may also consider seeing if any additional questions come to mind and asking them. Or, if you don't know where to start, try using the Journey Framework to ask helpful questions.

Here's what they might look like:

Face the Challenge

- Is there something I need to know about testing 4 out of 10 for feeling valuable?

- Is there anything I need to understand about testing 0 out of 10 for feeling resilient? (Feel free to customize these, of course.)

Listen for an answer or find a resource that can provide a list to test through that may be helpful. It could be a list of emotions or beliefs, your current to-do's, or difficult experiences from your past. Remember to be patient with yourself as you learn how to find these answers.

You could also ask something like:

- Do I have any emotions stuck in me that are influencing my self-worth?

- Did getting teased in school contribute to feeling less safe or powerless?

- Do I have any inherited subconscious paradigms causing this weakness?

Learn the Lesson

- Is there a message in this information for me?

Give your subconscious a moment to answer and pay attention to any thoughts that surface. Muscle test through ideas you have. Narrow down the possibilities through what feels right or wrong. Your mind and heart really do want you to succeed and be happy, so they will try to tell you what you need to understand. You may also identify clues to the changes that need to be made.

You could also ask something specific:

- Do I need to forgive (insert name here) for being unkind?

- Do I need to work on seeing myself differently, more positively than I have been?

- Is there something I need to learn or a story I need to know about from my family history?

Make the Change

- Is there something I can do about this?

Now find the action steps you need to take to change those numbers. Identify the behaviors or tasks that can help you build your self-worth or resilience (or whatever you tested weak for) and act on them. If the external direction tests weak, ask about any internal shifts that need to happen.

You could ask questions like:

- Are there any emotions I need to process?

- Are there beliefs I need to resolve?

- Can I strengthen those perceptions of value and resilience with my intention?

These are just a few of the types of questions that you can ask to gain valuable insights into your personal wellbeing. Hold onto what you learn here and we can begin resolving them in the next chapter.

We can easily shift these questions to professional issues as well.

- Test to see how strongly you believe that you can be successful in business. 0-10?

- Ask how strong your sense of power and influence is to make money. 0-10?

- How strong does it test when you ask about your purpose in serving the world with your unique gifts? 0-10?

- And, how capable do you feel you are to actually do so? 0-10?

Now evaluate the answers you tested for. Seek understanding about what you learned from your subconscious. Then, discover what actions you need to take to make the necessary changes.

Another approach to finding good questions to ask is to consider different ways of describing what you're experiencing. Find different words that trigger a new way to think about your concern. It can be a line from a book or an insight from a TED talk. Reframing what you're feeling or thinking can give you a new set of questions to consider to go deeper and gain powerful insights about your challenge.

Here's a juicy question to ask regarding a variety of topics.

- Is everything inside me in alignment with _____? Finish this question with things like: my health goals, my financial goals, my success goals, being happy, feeling peaceful, my value, my power, my resilience, my purpose, and so on.

This is a way to identify any internal blocks you may have for moving your life forward. Muscle testing through these for a *yes/no* answer can help you begin uncovering some mysteries that may have held you back from achieving your goals and dreams.

Changing these types of questions into statements and testing through to rate how strongly your subconscious believes them can open the door to resolving these types of blocks and limitations as well. They can give you a clear focus for strengthening them into powerful and productive beliefs that propel you toward success.

Here are some additional questions that may be helpful to get your mental juices flowing:

- Is there more than one factor contributing to my challenge?

- Is it best for me to do _____ (this task) first?

- Do I have a subconscious block to earning more money?

- Is it best for me to intervene in my children's argument?

- How good is it for me to take a break from working right now? Rate 0-10.

- Is it a good idea for me to eliminate sugar from my diet for a time? 1 day? 3 days? 1 week?

- Is it better for me to go read a book than take a nap right now?

- Is there anything else I need to know/learn about this challenge?

I hope you see how the world can open up to you with muscle testing and asking good questions. So much information is just waiting for you to tap into and uncover the mysteries of what has caused so many of your challenges.

CHAPTER 12

Making Internal Changes

Muscle testing is a very powerful way to discover what you need to know, learn the underlying messages, and identify what changes are necessary to overcome your challenges. Muscle testing can also be used to facilitate the actual change. It can not only help you identify the best external changes to make, but it can also facilitate internal shifts for improving mental, emotional, and physical wellbeing.

The process of testing doesn't make these changes; the strategies we employ do. Whether you use meditation, healing techniques, or other methods to resolve internal misalignments, muscle testing can assist you along the way. It can help you identify body systems that are malfunctioning, emotions that are stuck in you, beliefs that don't serve you anymore, and other root causes of issues you're facing.

This was certainly true for me. During the 18 years I struggled with my chronic illnesses, I searched, prayed, and worked hard to find the answers to overcome them. I learned remarkable things along the way about how our bodies really work. I learned about the variety of things that make us sick and the different parts of us that need attention in order for us to heal completely.

Muscle testing was a critical part of my journey over the last few months of healing. Once I learned how to test through the information in front of me, I would test not only for what was contributing to my issues, but also for the best way to heal them and, then, when they had resolved. I engaged fervently in the whole process and watched my efforts work miracles.

For the first time in 18 years, I was in control of how I was feeling. I could test for an unresolved emotion, release it, and feel immediate relief. The more I released, the more relief I felt. I couldn't believe what I was experiencing. For hours at a time, I sat on my bed testing, identifying, and healing emotions, then moving to the next one. I was hooked.

For so long, I had felt miserable and powerless. Then, I finally found the treasure I'd been seeking for nearly two decades, and I was on the home stretch. My body was healing and my life was about to change—I could feel it.

Each time I released an emotion, I would yawn. It was my body's merciful way of validating my efforts, so even when I didn't feel physical or emotional relief immediately, the yawn let me know I was still making progress. After the first few weeks of using this particular technique for releasing emotions, I discovered something that changed everything.

One day as I sat in my usual spot for my usual session, I tested to identify an emotion like normal, but I actually yawned *before* I did the technique. It surprised me, but I recognized quickly that something had happened. So, I tested and asked if I had released the emotion even though I hadn't done the technique. I tested *yes!* For a moment I just sat there, stunned. And honestly, I didn't quite know what to do with that information.

I took a breath and tested through some questions that slowly came to mind. What I wanted to know was how I had released the emotion without performing the technique. I learned through my earnest questioning that it's not about the technique we use for releasing and healing, it's our *intention*. This was a game changer for me for three reasons.

First, this was the first time I had needed to venture out to ask my own questions with muscle testing. I couldn't just test *yes* or *no* through a list of emotions to get the answers I needed. I took a step into the dark and asked questions I'd never considered before so I could learn what I needed to know. Muscle testing suddenly became a tool of discovery and change, not just one of identifying the next emotion to release.

That was the beginning of a whole new experience with muscle testing and asking questions. The focus moved beyond simply testing through and resolving emotions to learning and understanding the mysteries before me. It was intimidating, but I felt moved onto this new path, and that it would take me to the answers I needed in order to go beyond the healing I currently had access to.

Second, I learned through muscle testing (and prayer) that using my intention to shift things inside me was the real healing catalyst. The power was inside me, not in an external technique. I wasn't limited by someone's specific modality. I learned that my intention was the key to accessing all healing that is meant for me.

That led me to the third reason that understanding the power of intention was a game changer for me. I learned that I could not only release emotions, but also remove other blocks that were preventing me from fully healing. So, my focus became searching for resources to help me discover more comprehensive healing.

I muscle tested through several different resources that were relevant to my concerns and eventually compiled a few lists of things to test through regularly. I created lists of body systems with their structures and functions, energy systems that help healing energy flow through us, and lists of environmental factors that cause us to react.

It wasn't long before I created lists that were even deeper and more meaningful than those. They were lists of things that helped me learn about my purpose, my gifts, and how my subconscious affects everything.

The Surprising Results

By this point, I fully expected that personal, comprehensive healing was just around the corner. What I didn't expect was that this personal quest for deep healing would turn into a way to help *others* overcome *their* challenges. My efforts—muscle testing with better and better questions, prayer, and remarkable learning—became the basis for the techniques I teach in my book *Life Above the Line*.

I discovered that there are five areas where our bodies need nurturing in order to heal comprehensively. Those areas are physical, functional, energetic, vibrational, and genetic.

Very briefly (because I go into depth about these in my other book), we need to *heal* physically from injuries and tissue damage. We need to *strengthen* the functions within our bodies. We need to *remove* negative energetic influences. We need to *release* limiting beliefs, negative thoughts, and heavy emotions. And, we need to *restore* imprinted and inherited paradigms in our subconscious. This is the beginning to my approach to healing comprehensively.

All of this learning and healing was facilitated by muscle testing—I didn't have a keen intuition to draw from. Within just a handful of months, I didn't feel the constant pain anymore. I wasn't oppressively tired. All the random issues that came along with the chronic illnesses I had were gone. I healed! After 18 years, I had finally healed.

I was overwhelmed with gratitude. I knew God had led me through a miraculous journey so I could overcome my seemingly impossible challenges and then help others do the same.

My keys to healing were in some ways surprisingly simple— muscle testing, asking good questions, and resolving the root causes. I felt like Dorothy from *The Wizard of Oz* with her ruby slippers. I already had everything I needed to find my way home. I just had to go through the journey to know more about the challenges I was facing, learn the messages they were trying to teach me, and then be willing to change and heal. It was a massive chunk of my own journey through the *alchemy of becoming*. I became well. I became strong. And, I became a guide.

Now, I get to help you.

I'm glad you're here and that you've trusted me to guide you through learning the skill of muscle testing (and perhaps a bit more). I want to invite you now to practice using your new skill to help you make some internal changes. Let's apply it to not only gain important mental and emotional understanding, but also begin resolving those burdens.

If you already have techniques to overcome mental blocks and emotional burdens, use muscle testing to further your progress and deepen your transformation.

If you don't have any tools yet, I've created some simple yet powerful techniques, which I've referred to throughout this book, that I teach in my book *Life Above the Line* and in my audio programs. I want to share one of these techniques with you here: the vibrational release technique. It helps resolve limiting beliefs, negative thoughts, and emotional burdens.

Remember, the mind is more powerful than most of us realize. Our bodies listen carefully to each thought and respond accordingly—positively or negatively. This is a good thing. Even though it may seem like a burden depending upon where your life is now, it's actually a gift that allows you to change and improve the quality of your life. The power is in you!

From these positive or negative communications, our bodies then follow a path of building up or tearing down. Negative emotions and thoughts can lead to pain, illness, and other problematic symptoms or behaviors. Positive emotions and thoughts can lead to peace, healing, and strength.

Don't get discouraged if you're experiencing the fruits of past negativity or burdens. There's no judgement here. What this means is that you can employ your mind to help you heal. Here are some keys:

1. **Believe.** We must believe that it's possible to change and improve. Even if you don't feel like you have enough belief at this point, just hope it's possible and you're on your way.

2. **Be specific.** Just like with muscle testing, the more specific our desire is, the better the outcome. Thinking *I want to feel better* isn't as effective as thinking *I want to feel happier and more peaceful* or *I want to feel that I'm enough*.

3. **Clarify your intention.** This is how to gain control over an issue. Your intention is basically a combination of your belief, specific desire, and the energy to move it forward.

We put these keys to work with a simple process. Using just three steps, you can begin to change everything. Here's how it works.

Step 1: Choose the Issue

What issue would you like to focus on first? If you identified one or more in the last chapter, you can use one of them. I've also listed some options below to get you thinking. Read through them and listen to the thoughts that come or feelings that surface in your body to get your attention. You can also muscle test through the list, or the ideas that come to you, to identify which issue is ready to be resolved first. Just ask about each one at a time until you test *yes*.

1. A limiting belief: "I am powerless to change my life," "It is hard for me to make friends," "My family struggles with money."

2. A negative thought: "I am not good enough," "I will never be successful in business," "It's impossible for me to get out of debt," "I will never get to my goal weight."

3. A negative emotion: fear, regret, powerlessness, worthlessness, overwhelm, or whatever you're feeling that squashes you.

4. A painful memory: a heavy emotional event or trauma can add to our baggage

Step 2: Rate the Intensity

Rate the intensity of this issue on a scale from 1-10. We went through this earlier. It is purely subjective to help you keep track of your progress. You can sense how intense the issue is or muscle test through the numbers to identify its intensity.

Remember, you can ask if it's between 5 and 10 and then narrow down from there until you test *yes*. If you focus on an issue that's at least a 7 or 8 in intensity, it will be easier to feel and to recognize the shift more clearly as the intensity drops. We'll evaluate afterward to account for the shift.

Step 3: Think the word RELEASE

The word RELEASE is an effective word to use because we're working to eliminate beliefs, thoughts, and emotions that get stuck in us, creating drag. There is no magic in the word itself; our intentions give it the meaning and power to free us from these types of issues.

If a different word resonates better with you, use it. The word just gives your intention something to focus on—to help you accomplish this specific goal. The intention is to let go of or eliminate the root cause that's keeping the belief, thought, emotion, or memory stuck in you and holding you back.

So, think RELEASE now calm the intensity of your issue.

Step 4: Breathe

Breathing can help us move the energy and recognize the internal shift. It also helps us feel the intensity of our problem diminish. Now, think RELEASE and breathe.

Step 5: Repeat

Repeat steps 3 and 4 until you feel some relief and your issue calms down. You can test periodically through the process to recognize the shift in intensity. RELEASE and breathe.

How did it go? Check in to see how intense the issue is. Does it still bother you. If it has calmed down sufficiently, try another issue you're concerned about. Identify it, rate it, and release it.

If it hasn't calmed down, this is where the Journey Framework can be really helpful.

Face the Challenge

- Do I need to know anything else about this issue? *Yes* or *no?*

If *yes*, test through some thoughts or lists of emotions, or whatever you have handy, to help you discover what you're dealing with.

If *no*, ask yourself the next question.

Learn the Lesson

- Is there a lesson I need to learn from my challenge? *Yes* or *no?*

If *yes*, listen for a moment to hear what your mind, heart, or body is trying to tell you. Muscle test through the thoughts and feelings that come to confirm the lesson you need to learn.

If *no*, ask yourself the next question.

Make the Change

- Is there a change I need to make. *Yes* or *no?*

If *yes*, ask if the change is external. *Yes* or *no?*

If the answer is *yes*, consider what types of external, environmental, physical, or behavioral changes you need to make. If a lot of thoughts come to you, write them down. Then, test through to see which one or ones are right.

If the answer is *no*, ask if the change you need to make is internal. *Yes* or *no?*

If *yes*, walk through the technique again to see if you can make a change now.

If you don't feel relief or satisfaction about what you learned or changed, like there's still more for you to receive from this challenge, you can ask another question.

- Is there something else I need to know about this challenge? *Yes* or *no?*

Maybe there are more insights you need to gain. Maybe there is another lesson in it for you. Maybe there's more to heal.

The process of learning and growing and changing is fluid and constant. Go through the Journey Framework and the healing technique as often as you need.

This is alchemy in action. We have the choice to go through our challenges intentionally and allow them to help us grow and become the best versions of ourselves. Choose to engage in this beautiful process. Be patient with yourself and be open to new understanding and opportunities to find more health, happiness, and success.

In the next chapter, you'll learn how to set yourself up for success by creating customized resources for continued growth, things that can help you identify important factors contributing to your challenge. They can help you get the messages your life is trying to give you. And, they can empower you to make necessary life-changing adjustments both around and inside of you.

Chapter 13

Creating Your Own Resources

Sometimes it's easy to understand and break down our challenges, ask clear and simple questions, and get helpful, guiding answers. But sometimes it's overwhelming, like trying to find a single needle hidden in a field full of haystacks. It's not *if* this will happen to you, it's *when*. And when it does, you will need a good strategy to guide your questions and simplify your approach. Good lists and other defined resources can help narrow your search and hone your skills for seeking answers to any challenge.

There are so many resources that you can test through in order to learn important information regarding your wellbeing and your life—what you react to, what you should focus on, where underlying issues are, and things to resolve. In Chapter 6: Using Your Resources, you learned how to find lists in books, on websites, and items in your home, etc. Now let's talk more about how to compile your own lists and resources so they can be most helpful to you.

At the beginning of my muscle-testing journey, I basically lived off of other people's lists. I still appreciate the time and thought that some very talented and well-meaning people put into the lists they created. But I soon found that other people's resources, no matter how well done, were missing things that I needed to help me learn and progress.

Because I had received so much value from those lists, at first I felt a little presumptuous about making my own. But as I stepped forward into my own list making, I realized very quickly that my hesitations were unnecessary. Lists are simply tools and, as the lists improve, they become more effective instruments in helping us along our journey.

This is where creating your own lists can be invaluable. They can contain anything from your favorite foods, books, movies, activities, places, or even people (really!). They can focus on health, personal development, and more. The possibilities are truly limitless. All these things can provide helpful insights as you strive to overcome your challenges.

I have created a lot of lists along the way, most of which I gleaned from multiple sources. I made sure these valuable nuggets of information were organized and easily accessible, because I referenced them often. As I began using muscle testing in a focused way to heal from my illnesses, the most important lists I created were of body systems, including the most common organs, structures, and functions; many common environmental elements that I often reacted to; and customized lists of emotions, thoughts, and beliefs.

I also noticed that I was reacting to a lot of different foods and nature in general. So I created lists to help me understand what my body wasn't liking. My food list contains a variety of foods, including fruits, vegetables, nuts, seeds, grains, meats, dairy, sweeteners, beans, fats, herbs, condiments, and more. While not a comprehensive list, it's been a great resource for myself and my clients.

My nature list was more general—grass, weather, temperature, etc.—but it has grown to include all sorts of factors found in my personal environment, such as things (and people) that bring stress into my life.

While creating your own lists to test through can take some time, the focused effort you put in now will save you a lot of time later on when you are ready to dig in and find answers. If you already know what lists would be meaningful to you, start working on them. You can also refer to the ideas at the end of this chapter.

To help you get going, here are my top 3 tips for creating customized lists:

1. Identify what kinds of lists are relevant to you. Maybe you need to identify things that you are experiencing reactions to. Perhaps your list needs to contain resources that help you understand better what you're thinking and feeling. You may even need a list of activities you enjoy for when you're feeling down.

Muscle testing through these kinds of lists can remove emotions and biases to help you make decisions for what is best for you in each situation.

Do you have a list of favorite quotes? A list like this could help you learn lessons that your challenges are trying to teach you. It could be full of wisdom or encouragement or comfort.

The beauty of preparing lists for yourself is that it's giving yourself the gift of easily accessible guidance and meaningful insights when you need them most.

2. Identify helpful sources to draw from. Once you decide what type of list you need, take the time to gather helpful resources in order to create it. Again, these can come from books, websites, your cupboards, etc. Looking through the bookshelves, kitchen cupboards, or refrigerators of supportive friends and family can also be a great resource for new ideas. (This can lead to some wonderful conversations!)

Sometimes the only resource you need is your own mind and intuition. Some of the lists you need to create may simply require that you to sit quietly and listen for a few minutes. Then, write down the thoughts that come.

Every now and then, a list is clear and easy to compile, no muscle testing necessary. It can be helpful, however, to know when you need to add more ideas to your list and when it's complete. When there is so much material to work with that it becomes confusing and difficult, it is then that muscle testing is essential to narrow down the resources and options that will be most useful in creating the list.

That was my experience as I began making my lists for body systems and foods and such. I wasn't sure where to start. I looked at the resources I had around me—books on my shelves, websites, and images online—and found so many sources that I had to narrow them down so I wasn't overwhelmed.

3. Identify elements to include in your lists. Once I had narrowed down these resources through muscle testing, I began evaluating their similarities and differences. I then tested through to determine which individual items I should keep and which to set aside.

What I found was that there were a lot of common pieces that obviously needed to be included on my list, but then I also tested that I should specifically include and exclude certain things to create the best list for me.

Some of the things I discovered were rather surprising. For example, there are differing opinions about some organs and functions belonging to certain body systems, such as glands. Who knew there were so many differing opinions about how to categorize glands! When I came to conundrums like this, I simply tested where and how I should group them for my particular wellbeing.

You may also find that many existing resources don't account for things that seem obvious. When I was making my food chart, I included herbs and condiments, even though most food charts I found didn't list them. These items have been an extremely helpful addition to my food list, as I had reactions to some of them that I may not have discovered otherwise.

After you compile your list, place the items in order if it makes sense to—alphabetically, chronologically, numerically, etc. Then number them. It is easier to muscle test through a numbered list than a group of words. It's similar to testing through 0-10 to rate something. You simply break it down into a range of numbers and narrow down until you identify the correct number.

When you think you've finished compiling your list, muscle test and ask a very simple yet valuable question:

- Is there anything else that needs to go on my list?

If *yes*, ask questions to find them. If *no*, you're good to go!

I invite you to consider all types of lists that can hold value for you. Whether you're looking for answers to health challenges, going after a goal, or seeking more meaning in your life, you can create lists that facilitate this kind of healing, achieving, and enlightenment. Muscle testing can lead you through powerful transformations if you face your challenges, learn the lessons inside them, and make the necessary changes to move your life forward.

To help you get started, here are 20 ideas for lists you could create. Read through these suggestions and see if anything stands out as particularly helpful in your journey right now. Then muscle test to evaluate and confirm what you should focus on first. Once you identify where to start, pull out your phone, your computer, or a piece of paper and get to work!

Types of lists to consider:

1. Foods - healthy, unhealthy, and everything in between
2. Natural remedies - essential oils, herbal supplements, homeopathics
3. Body parts - Don't be shy here. Write down everything that can be helpful.
4. Body system functions - Yes, body system functions are separate from the body parts themselves.
5. Emotions - You can create an uplifting list or a list to identify burdensome emotions.
6. Areas of your life - personal, professional, purpose, spiritual, relationships, etc. Lists like this are super helpful when trying learn messages from your challenges.
7. Priorities - List your top 10 or so, and then test to put them in order of priority.
8. The 5 (or 6) Senses - I include intuition in my list of senses.
9. Colors - Yes, people can react to colors.
10. Current issues or projects - family concerns, finances, remodeling, book writing ;)

11. World events - world or national issues, natural disasters, crime
12. Pathogens/organisms - viruses, bacteria, parasites
13. Energy systems - meridians, chakras, aura
14. Nutrients - vitamins, minerals, proteins, carbohydrates, fats, fibre, water
15. Elements in nature - trees, insects, animals, weather
16. Places you go often - home, church, work, store, park
17. Regular activities - exercise, dating, sports, hobbies
18. Menus - family dinners, special diets, weight loss
19. Quotes - uplifting, inspiring, empowering, thought-provoking
20. Books - personal development, cookbooks, how-to, fiction

CHAPTER 14

Embracing the Journey

The journey to reach your full potential in this life is personal, profound, and perfect. No one else can live life for you—it's yours to lead, and the challenges are yours to face. The lessons life offers you will nurture and teach you everything that's needed to become who you're meant to become. Every invitation to change provides the exact stepping stone you need along the path to lift you to your full potential and do what you're meant to do.

The gift of muscle testing and asking quality questions can guide you through every twist and turn in life. Understanding more clearly your weaknesses and strengths will empower you to navigate every challenge you face.

Personal

Your personal experience through life's alchemy is yours. It belongs to you. No one else can live your life for you. No one can make your choices for you, grow for you, or change for you. Only you can become you.

Your challenges aren't random. They are individual and unique to you. I've seen so many times where a person's challenges—faced and overcome—have made that person blossom into a more genuine version of themselves and their previously hidden gifts begin to shine.

The journey of life is difficult. If it weren't, it wouldn't have the power to metabolize your struggles, heartaches, illnesses— you name it—into strengths. It wouldn't give you sufficient motivation to change, grow, and improve. Only through the necessary effort and sacrifice can you reach your full potential.

This *alchemy of becoming* is mirrored in the creation of diamonds. A diamond doesn't become a diamond without intense pressure, incredible heat, and a really long time exposed to both. This is our destiny—to become like diamonds. So, we must experience this kind of refinement.

Begin to see your challenges as gifts and opportunities to discover new levels of peace, joy, health, and success. Choose to engage in the process and accept every trial and problem as a clue to an answer you've been seeking. Dive into its secrets to discover the prize inside meant just for you.

Profound

Life is a series of classrooms and lessons to learn in. Whether it's actually in school or the school of life, this life is filled with profound messages of wisdom and growth. The sooner you learn how to listen and learn, the smoother life can go.

Learning life's messages when they whisper can often help to deter more intense difficulties while still receiving their wisdom. It's when those subtle messages are ignored out of busyness or fear, or whatever, that it can result in unnecessary pain.

Because your potential is so great and there is so much you can do to help others around you through life and its challenges, your very being is wired for profound learning and growth. Life is a journey that offers deep relationships, remarkable knowledge, and beautiful opportunities to reach beyond your present understanding of yourself to a higher and nobler vision of you—who you really are.

You are meant to have a profound impact on the world. Your challenges are keys to understanding that truth and becoming the kind of person who can make that kind of impact.

Perfect

Your journey through life is perfect—that is, whole, complete, and pertinent. It's perfect in its pain, its trauma, and its blessings. It's just right in its intensity and duration, lessons and limitations. Our growth in life is marked with traumas and triumphs, and it is the blood, sweat, and tears we shed that glisten in the light. It is the dark areas that allow the bright bits to sparkle.

You cannot fully know joy without difficulty. You cannot know real peace without the chaos. It is the dichotomy of life's ups and downs that allows you to breathe in and out, find meaning, and strive for more.

Welcome deep change when life offers it to you. Don't shy away from opportunities to reevaluate your reality—what and who is around you. Embrace the big and small changes that nudge you out of your comfort zone and into a space of creating new strength.

As you work toward becoming your best self and reaching your potential, you become more capable of living a meaningful life. You get better at discovering your gifts and talents that will help you fulfill your purpose. I believe you have a unique and beautiful purpose to fulfill, which includes ways to serve others, lift them, and help them experience greater health, joy, love, and success.

The better and more skilled you become at life's alchemy of facing your challenges, learning the lessons life is trying to teach you, and changing in ways that make you better each day, the more power you will have over the quality of your life.

There will be less struggle because you are willing to learn and grow, less heartache because you know you will become stronger through the pain, and less anger because you are grateful for the opportunity to discover a better way to live.

With each difficulty you face in your life, I invite you to use muscle testing and the Journey Framework to discover the answers you need to embrace your unique adventure. They will guide your efforts to seek understanding for the personal challenges you face, help you learn the profound lessons that invite you to grow, and empower you to make the necessary changes that move your life forward perfectly and help you achieve your full potential.

You are worth every effort it takes to become the diamond that you are meant to be.

I'm rooting for you!

APPENDIX:

TESTING LISTS

QUESTIONS TO ASK

Sometimes one of the biggest challenges to getting started is knowing which questions to ask. For your convenience, nearly every question in this book is listed below to help you find and formulate the right questions for you to ask in any given moment.

As you test through the following questions, customize them to your situation. Trade out words or phrases to make them pertinent to you. Find your preferences of wording in the repeated questions. Honestly seek out the information you need to know to help you move forward in your life.

FACE THE CHALLENGE

1. Is there something I need to know about this issue?
2. Is there more than one factor contributing to my challenge?
3. Do I need to know anything more about the issue itself?
4. Is it in any of my resources?
5. Is there something we can or need to know about it?
6. Is there anything else I need to know about contributing factors?
7. Is there anything else I need to know?
8. Is there more we need to know there?
9. Is there more I need to know before I receive a message?
10. Is there a chapter in this book that I need to review, find something in, study more deeply, etc.?
11. Is what I need to know on any testing pages?
12. Is there a particular factor we need to identify about the catch in the other swings?

13. Is there something I need to know about testing 4 out of 10 for feeling valuable?
14. Is there anything I need to understand about testing 0 out of 10 for feeling resilient?

LEARN THE LESSON

1. Is there a lesson I need to learn from my challenges?
2. Is there a message in this concern—a lesson I need to learn?
3. Is there a lesson in my muscle tightness?
4. Is there a message behind this issue?
5. Is there a message in this information for me?
6. Is there a lesson or a message I need to understand?
7. Is there a lesson I need to learn?
8. What else do I need to know? (Listen for an answer.)
9. Is that part of the lesson I need to understand?
10. Is there any other message I need to understand from this?
11. Is there anything else I can learn about this?
12. Is there a chapter in this book that can help me learn a message I need?
13. What does that mean to me? (Listen for an answer.)
14. Is there something I need to learn or a story I need to know about from my family history?
15. Is there anything else I need to know/learn about this challenge?

MAKE THE CHANGE

1. Is there a change that needs to be made?
2. Is there something I can do to help this?
3. Is it external / behavioral?
4. Externally? Internally?
5. Does something internal that needs to be resolved?

6. Is there anything I need to do internally to help resolve the issue?

7. Are there any emotions I need to process?

8. Are there beliefs I need to resolve?

9. Can I strengthen those perceptions of value and resilience with my intention?

10. Is there something in this book that can help me make needed changes?

11. What chapter has a clue to what change I need to make?

12. Do I need to review the Practice chapter?

13. Is there anything else to resolve?

14. Is there anything else I need to know, learn, or change about this tightness?

15. Do I need to forgive (insert name here) for being unkind?

16. Do I need to work on seeing myself differently, more positively than I have been?

UNIVERSAL

1. Is water good for me?

2. My name is…

3. You may state your eye or hair color.

4. You could reference being inside or outside.

5. Is it okay to ask this question?

6. What question do I really need to ask?

7. Do I need to use the Journey Framework to help me with my issue?

8. How strong/intense is this issue? 0-10

9. Is everything inside me in alignment with _____? Finish this question with things like: my health goals, my financial goals, my success goals, being happy, feeling peaceful, my value, my power, my resilience, my purpose, and so on.

10. Is it best for me to do _____ (this task) first?

11. Is there a muscle testing list I need to create right now?
12. Test through the suggested lists in Chapter 13 for what list you need to create first.
13. Is there anything else that needs to go on my list?

FAMILY

1. Does it have something to do with my kids?
2. Do I need to be more generous with my time toward my family?
3. Is it best for me to intervene in my children's argument?

FOOD/NUTRITION

1. Is the root cause of this reaction to dairy physical?
2. Is the root cause of the reaction emotional?
3. Is it best for me to eat an apple right now?
4. Do I need any supplements this morning?
5. Does my body need more water today?
6. Will I have a reaction to this food?
7. Am I having a reaction to the apple I ate?
8. Do I need more Vitamin C in my diet?
9. Is it best for me to eat an apple today?
10. Do I need more protein in my diet?
11. Am I hungry?
12. Is it good for me to eat sugar all day?
13. Is it a good idea for me to eliminate sugar from my diet for a time? 1 day? 3 days? 1 week?

GOALS/PURPOSE/PROFESSION

1. Is it right, according to my personal path and purpose, to develop these skills so I can help my family through any challenge?

2. I feel resistance in moving toward my goal; do I need to understand something?
3. Does it have something to do with work?
4. Does it have to do with the new expectations on me at work?
5. Do I have a book in my personal library that can help me move toward my goals?
6. Is it best to watch an inspirational video someone suggested recently?
7. Do I need to be braver about reaching for my dreams?
8. Am I fully committed to doing what it takes to improve the quality of my life?
9. Am I all-in to reaching my goal?
10. Test to see how strongly you believe that you can be successful in business. 0-10?
11. Ask how strong your sense of power and influence is to make money. 0-10?
12. How strong does it test when you ask about your purpose in serving the world with your unique gifts? 0-10?
13. And, how capable do you feel you are to actually do so? 0-10?
14. Do I have a subconscious block to earning more money?
15. How good is it for me to take a break from working right now? Rate 0-10.
16. I will never be successful in business. Rate 0-10.
17. It's impossible for me to get out of debt. 0-10?

PHYSICAL HEALTH

1. Is it best for me to exercise for 20 minutes today?
2. Is it best for me to go for a walk today?
3. Is it best to exercise for more than 15 minutes? or 30 minutes?

4. Do I need to get more sleep?
5. Do I need to go to bed earlier?
6. Is it better for me to go read a book than take a nap right now?
7. I will never get to my goal weight. (How strong does it test? 0-10?)

PAIN/DISCOMFORT

1. Is there something I need to know about my stomachache?
2. Does my stomach hurt because of something I ate?
3. Does it hurt because I'm getting sick?
4. Does it hurt because I'm feeling anxious about something?
5. Is there anything else I need to know about why my stomach hurts?
6. Is there something I need to know about the pain I keep feeling in my neck or back or feet, etc.?
7. Is there something I need to know about the tightness in my muscles?
8. Is there an emotion contributing to the tightness? Is there another emotion?
9. Does the muscle tightness cause me to feel that way?

MENTAL/EMOTIONAL WELLBEING

1. Is there an emotion underlying my discomfort?
2. Am I being limited in my success by a negative belief about myself?
3. Is my impatience adding to my stress today?
4. Do I have any inherited patterns limiting my happiness?
5. Is it helpful to identify why I'm feeling anxious?
6. Am I peaceful?
7. Am I stressed about something?

8. Am I willing to learn?
9. Do I feel confident?
10. Do I need to entertain positive instead of negative thoughts?
11. Do I need to be kinder to that grumpy co-worker?
12. Do I feel truly free?
13. Do I have a limiting belief about being able to improve my life?
14. Does golf have anything to do with pessimism or despair?
15. Am I feeling any despair about golf?
16. Can I isolate what's happening to limit the other swings?
17. I am valuable. (How strongly does your subconscious believe this statement? 0-10?)
18. I have a strong influence over my life. (How strong does it test? 0-10?)
19. I am resilient. (How strong is this for you? 0-10?)
20. I have purpose. (How strong? 0-10?)
21. Do I have any emotions stuck in me that are influencing my self-worth?
22. Did getting teased in school contribute to feeling less safe or powerless?
23. Do I have any inherited subconscious paradigms causing this weakness?
24. Do I have a heavy emotional event or trauma that is adding to my emotional baggage?
25. I am powerless to change my life. (How strong does it test? 0-10?)
26. It is hard for me to make friends. (How strong is this? 0-10?)
27. My family struggles with money. (How strong? 0-10?)
28. I am not good enough. (How strong does it test? 0-10?)

EMOTIONS

DIFFICULT

1. Abandoned
2. Afraid
3. Angry
4. Anxious
5. Apathetic
6. Avoiding
7. Bitter
8. Burdened
9. Closed
10. Conceited
11. Confused
12. Defensive
13. Depressed
14. Disconnected
15. Discouraged
16. Embarrassed
17. Frustrated
18. Grieving
19. Hopeless
20. Nervous
21. Obsessed
22. Overwhelmed
23. Panicked
24. Powerless
25. Resentful
26. Self-pity
27. Shocked
28. Stubborn
29. Worthless

POSITIVE

1. Cherished
2. Courageous
3. Peaceful
4. Calm
5. Interested
6. Seeking
7. Agreeable
8. Light
9. Welcoming
10. Humble
11. Clear
12. Thoughtful
13. Happy
14. Connected
15. Encouraged
16. Composed
17. Patient
18. Comforted
19. Hopeful
20. Confident
21. Free
22. Optimistic
23. Trusting
24. Powerful
25. Grateful
26. Self-esteem
27. Steady
28. Flexible
29. Valuable

ABOUT THE AUTHOR

Tiffany Garvin is a #1 bestselling author of the life-changing book *Life Above the Line: Living the Life You're Meant to Live.*

She is an executive coach, international speaker, and innovator in the field of personal development. For eighteen years, she struggled with debilitating chronic illnesses. When she finally overcame that challenge, what she learned along the way became the catalyst for her life's work.

Her vision is to empower people around the world to harness their innate gifts and abilities to overcome their own challenges, live their genius, and create a life they love. Then, invite them to Serve, Love, and Lift those around them.

Despite her chronic illnesses, she graduated from Brigham Young University with a Bachelor of Arts degree in Asian Studies/Chinese and earned a first degree black belt in Kenpo Jiu jitsu. She is happily married, the mother of three children, and loves her life of coaching, speaking, and lifting people toward their potential.

www.TiffanyGarvin.com   www.ServeLoveLift.com

www.ingramcontent.com/pod-product-compliance
Lightning Source LLC
Chambersburg PA
CBHW072151270326
41930CB00011B/2390